BE POSITI\

How positive are you feeling today?

You might be full of optimism and confidence. Perhaps you're excited about an event that's coming up in your life. Or maybe it's the opposite and you're feeling unsure of yourself or worried about something you've got to do in the near future. When your mind is full of negative chatter and limiting beliefs, achieving success becomes a challenge.

While it's impossible to escape negativity entirely, you can learn to focus on the positive and use this optimistic mindset to help navigate the obstacles life will inevitably throw your way.

So, next time you feel self-conscious, worry that you're not going to be able to cope or just feel generally low, this book is here to help. Use what's written inside to get to grips with fears and doubts, discover what you can do to overcome them and move forward with confidence.

YOU CAN DO ANYTHING

CONTENTS

THINK POSITIVE

Do you feel able to take on the world? Seeing yourself in a positive light gives you enthusiasm for life, an inner confidence, a sense of what is right and, most importantly, a feeling that anything is possible

Do you believe in yourself? Do you feel sure of your strengths and abilities? Not in an arrogant, 'I'm so amazing' way, but in an honest one that means you know who you are and accept every part of yourself – the good and the bad. Because believing in yourself can be harder than you might think. Easy to say, but not so easy to do. Everyone struggles to feel secure in themselves at some point (in fact, many times) over their lifetime. It's simply part of being human.

Why it matters
If you have a positive outlook and believe that you are capable of whatever life throws at you, you feel more ready for life's experiences. You know you can rely on your abilities to handle challenges, and you are likely to embrace opportunities rather than shy away from them. And even when things don't go as planned, your belief in yourself can help you to try again. When you're faced with a task that you find tough, you think 'I can', or 'With practice I can', rather than 'I can't'.

Accepting the good

Has anyone ever told you that you're funny? That you're kind, or creative? Good at sport, at writing or that you work hard? Did you believe them when they said those things? When those around you notice your strengths and talents, it can give your confidence a boost – but only if you believe what they've said is actually true. Is that voice inside you friendly, encouraging you to accept it when someone says something nice about you? Or is it harsh and mean, making you doubt what they say? If so, then that's the opposite of believing in yourself.

Learning to believe

The best way to nurture the belief that you can do it, is through using the abilities that you have, learning, practising and, importantly, trying again when things don't work out. The more you do, the more you'll discover and see what you're truly capable of. When you focus on what you can do, you start to take pride in your achievements, and then your belief becomes even stronger.

THERE ARE SOME OTHER THINGS YOU CAN DO TO BOOST YOUR SELF-BELIEF

Choose friends wisely
Surround yourself with people who make you feel good about yourself. A lot of how you see yourself is based on how you think other people see you. Don't waste your time with people who aren't positive, and don't get too caught up with approval and reactions on social media.

Don't compare yourself to others
Everyone has their own strengths and weaknesses, and yours will be different to your friends'. Embrace everything about yourself, quirks and all, and you won't be wishing you were more like somebody else.

Be kind to yourself
When your inner voice is mean or negative, stop and say something positive instead. If it says, 'I can't', say 'I can'. If it says, 'I'll never be able to do it', say, 'With some hard work I can learn how to do this'.

Take some risks
Give new things a go, say yes when opportunities come up, try out for a team, raise your hand in class more often, say what you really think (as long as it won't hurt someone else's feelings!).

Be true to yourself
Only you know you. Feel confident in your actions and don't worry that you need to act a certain way to fit in with others. Don't be embarrassed about wanting to do your best, and never feel foolish for trying. Let others see you for who you are – mistakes, insecurities, the lot. When you don't feel you have to hide something you can't do well, suddenly it doesn't seem as important.

And remember... It takes courage to be the real you. The more honest you are about who you are, to yourself and to others, the more you will believe in yourself. It takes time to build, but keep at it.

OFF TO THE PERFECT START

Put a spring in your step with one-minute morning routines that will help you face your day with energy and positivity

Morning routines don't need to be time-consuming or complex to be effective. Here are seven one-minute exercises that can transform your day – and maybe even your whole life – if practised regularly.

1 Practise gratitude

Choose to start your day with a positive emotion by reflecting on the things you appreciate most. You can do this before you've even opened your eyes and are still tucked up under your sheets. Take a moment to think about the thing or person you are most grateful for in your life right now. Notice the feeling you get when you do this. Once you've thought of one, keep going until you have three. It's not what you list that's important – it could be anything from your friends to your morning smoothie – but rather the feeling you get when you think of it.

Practising gratitude every day will rewire your brain for happiness by training it to focus on the positive, rather than the negative. Don't worry if you find it challenging at first, the more you do it, the easier it will get.

2 Breathe with your heart

Before your mind starts racing with all the things you need to do that day, take a moment to pause and reconnect with your breath and with your heart. Close your eyes and place your hand on your heart, focusing your attention there. Breathe deeply as though your breath is moving in and out of your heart area. Begin to regulate your breathing to a count of six – breathing in to your heart space for six seconds and breathing out for six seconds. Repeat this pattern for one minute. Bringing awareness to your breath in this way and slowing down your heart rate with longer breaths can help you feel calmer and more relaxed. You can repeat this technique throughout the day if you become overwhelmed by a task or emotion.

3 Daily affirmations

Daily affirmations can become a key part of your morning routine, used to counteract negative self-talk and reprogramme your subconscious towards more empowering, positive beliefs. First you need a good understanding of what your limiting beliefs are – it could be 'I'm terrible at presenting my ideas in front of a group of people', for example. Ask yourself when you first believed this. How true is it – do other people think this too or is it just you? What impact is holding onto this belief having on your life? How much do you want to change it? What's stopping you from believing something different?

If you're sure this belief is holding you back in some way and you're determined to change it by taking action, write an affirmation that is the positive opposite of your current belief – in this case: 'I am good at public speaking'. If that feels unrealistic, tweak the affirmation until it is believable – for example: 'I am getting better at public speaking by practising regularly'. As you begin to improve you can change the affirmation again. So, it might be: 'I am getting good at public speaking' – until you reach a point where you believe the positive opposite of your original belief. So 'I am no good at public speaking' eventually becomes 'I am good at public speaking'.

Once you have your affirmation repeat it to yourself for one minute every morning, allowing the words fully to sink in. Then continue to say it throughout the day, as many times as you like. This will support you in taking action towards your goal and your new belief by reprogramming your subconscious mind. You may find saying your affirmation in the mirror makes it even more powerful.

4 Write it down

Whether it's a list of things you need to do that day or a stream of consciousness, getting muddled thoughts out of your head and onto the page will help you process them more easily. Journalling gives you a safe space that is non-judgmental. It may even help you find meaning and insights from your experiences that might not have otherwise come to light – you could be surprised at what comes out when you put pen to paper.

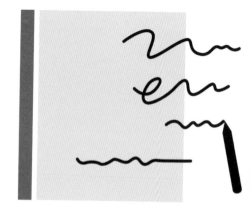

5 Hydrate yourself

It may sound simple, but starting the day by drinking a glass of water will fire up your metabolism, help your body flush out any toxins and rehydrate you – after all, you did just go the whole night without drinking anything at all. Taking on water first thing in the morning means your brain doesn't have to struggle against the effects of dehydration and it will help you to start the day thinking more clearly.

6 Mindful showering

Mindfulness doesn't have to be practised while sitting cross-legged on a beach, as an online image search may have you believe. It can be practised anytime, anywhere, by bringing the focus of your attention into the present moment. You can even do this while showering. Focus your attention on the water as it splashes onto your skin and, once you're fully present with the sensation, bring in a cleansing meditation by imagining all your worries being washed down the drain.

7 Get up and get down

Whether it's a few stretches as you sit up in bed, a full-on sun salutation or a dance around your bedroom to your favourite tune, moving your body first thing in the morning will help you feel energised and will also kick-start your mind, improving your focus and mental abilities throughout the day. Even if it feels silly at first, dancing to a guilty pleasure is a sure way to boost your mood for the day ahead.

BODY LANGUAGE

Did you know that the way you stand, hold yourself and move can affect your mood and the way others see you too?

Your body tells a fascinating story. It's not just the obvious things such as size, shape, hair and teeth that give clues to the kind of life you've lived so far – the way you hold your body and how it moves can also tell people a lot about how you're feeling inside.

Want to know how someone feels? Look at their posture and movement. Curious about how your body movement could affect your mind? Read on to find out how small yet powerful changes could make a big difference from head to toe.

Body talk

The idea of body language is something that has evolved over thousands of years, and the way it works differs from culture to culture. Some gestures are governed by nature, such as a smile or laugh, whereas others have evolved with society – good and bad table manners, for instance.

When thinking of body language, the focus is usually on how the body speaks to the people around you. Do you look confident and capable, or weak and unsure? Are you truthful or deceiving, vulnerable or dominant? Non-verbal communications like eye contact can send silent messages about you. The way your body speaks to you, however, is even more important. Posture, rate of breathing, tense muscles and even simple acts like walking affect the brain and suggest which hormones, chemicals and mood signals to send out. And it's a two-way street. Your mood can also lead to poor posture, and before you know it, a cycle of hunched shoulders, low mood and muscle tension has built up. But there are ways to stop this cycle, or at least put it on pause, and see the impact it has on your mood and mind.

Shoulders back

You might have been told to 'stand up straight with your shoulders back'. This simple message might sound like something your parents, or even Mary Poppins, would say, but the act of standing up straight with the shoulders back is a silent signal of confidence, power and belief in oneself. Think of how stars like Beyoncé stand and present themselves on stage. And it doesn't just work for humans. Scientific studies have shown that even the humble lobster changes its posture depending upon whether it wins or loses a fight. The lobster that comes top stretches itself out and opens up its body, while the loser hunches down and appears smaller. Researchers have discovered the larger, triumphant posture is linked to a release of chemicals that boost mood and confidence. Meanwhile, the smaller, hunched posture is more commonly associated with defeat and having less energy.

Back on dry land, you may notice how your posture changes according to your current situation. Simply walking tall and openly is far more likely to generate positive social interactions and agreement from others. Hunching over is a silent signal to everyone around you that something is wrong.

Posture and mood are linked on a level so deep it's easy to overlook. Many cultures emphasise a good diet, exercise and education, but fail to address the results of hunched shoulders, a downward gaze, tight stomach muscles or a clenched jaw.

Hormone boost

A recent study has even found that memory recall is affected by posture. People sitting in a slouched position found it easier to remember negative memories, while positive memories were easier to recall when sitting upright.

The researchers also noted that hormone levels were linked to posture. A slouched position was seen to increase cortisol (also known as the stress hormone) and decrease testosterone, and an upright posture to increase testosterone while decreasing cortisol. Testosterone is partly responsible for encouraging good mood levels, decreasing body fat, strengthening the heart and bones, and decreasing irritability and tiredness, so when it comes to lifting your mood, it could be useful to think about how you've been standing and sitting recently.

Serotonin is another hormone – found in both lobsters and humans – that is associated with happiness, relaxation and a sense of security. Low serotonin levels are often accompanied by anxiety and depression, while stable and balanced levels allow for satisfaction, a sense of security and a greater ability to think long-term and plan for the future. It is also released or held back depending upon posture.

Standing up tall with the shoulders back sends a silent signal that you're open to and can handle the world, helping levels of serotonin flow more freely throughout the body and brain. In turn, this can help to enhance feelings of wellbeing and balance mood levels.

HEAD-TO-TOE TIPS

Head
The mind is a storehouse of memories, which means many movement patterns are down to past experiences, telling the body how to move. Spend some time observing how you move. Do you take big or small strides? Are your shoulders too tight? Do your hands tend to be clenched fists? Does your stomach tie itself in a knot when you think about a certain subject or when you're preparing for a particular activity?

Lungs
Shallow breathing is a sure-fire way to block sensations and emotions from forming and flowing freely and signals to the brain that something is wrong. A few moments of slow and conscious breathing each day can help tremendously, especially when it comes to calming any worried thoughts.

Stomach
Holding in the belly can affect relaxation and prevent the body from working optimally, and allowing these muscles to relax is one way to ease tension and feel calm. It's also an easy tool to use daily. An exercise to try for yourself is to sit or lie down and practise consciously relaxing the stomach, breathing slowly and deeply so you can feel the breath moving into the lungs and ribcage, allowing the belly to expand too. A couple of minutes of breathing in this way can be a quick and simple way to send those silent signals to the body that it's perfectly fine to relax.

Hips
When Colombian singer Shakira famously sang 'hips don't lie', she was right. The muscles around the hips have an effect upon the diaphragm via the psoas muscle. They also help to shape the body's overall posture. Tight hip flexors pull the body into a hunched position, but gently stretching the thighs, hips and lower back can help relieve the physical tightness and any accompanying emotional tension.

Feet
All the way down at the feet, it's time to take a look at those toes. Ill-fitting shoes can cause the toes to scrunch up together, making balance more difficult, even when it comes to walking. Feeling unsteady on your feet causes the rest of the body to tighten and lock up, so practising walking barefoot and spreading the toes can help work towards the ultimate goal – a more balanced body and mind.

SUCCESS IS WHAT YOU MAKE IT

Here's how to set goals and win at life, whatever that looks like for you

Take a moment to think of a successful person. What do you picture? Is it a person with top-class grades? The captain of your school sports team? A YouTuber with more than half a million followers? It can often seem that to be successful you need to be rich, beautiful or super-popular.

It's an idea often reinforced by magazines, films and social media. Even the *Oxford English Dictionary* states that success is someone with 'fame, wealth or social status'. It's no wonder the word makes many people feel anxious. It also begs the question: if you're not rich, beautiful or super-popular, are you unsuccessful?

The answer is NO. And with capital letters, too, as it's that important to remember. The *Oxford English Dictionary* also defines success as 'a person or thing that achieves desired aims', which is a much healthier and more realistic way to approach the concept. Just in case the media, the movie-makers and social media superpowers have all forgotten, it's worth restating: we're all unique, with different desires, aims and ideas of what it means to do well.

Do you want to start your own business doing something creative? Is your dream to travel the world and save the seas? Do you want to work with people less fortunate than you? Or have a farm? Or a fashion brand? Or a big family? Whatever you long for in life, the true meaning of success is to go out there and make it happen.

Who cares if your nail-art salon doesn't mean you get to travel everywhere by private jet? Or if that awesome dog-grooming job means you're not living what others would consider a glamorous life. And so what if working as a nurse in emergency medicine won't win you a string of gold awards? The point is to strive for what makes you happy, and be proud to know that what you're working towards is your own dream, not one fed to you by the media or Hollywood (or even your family and teachers).

If you're not sure what you even want to achieve yet, that's okay, too. There are only a handful of people who know their true passion at a young age. In fact, it can take decades to find out what you're interested in, so don't feel under pressure. Think about the things you'd like to do more of – draw, dance, spend time with animals, make people laugh – and start from there. Who knows, you could end up being a comedian, an illustrator or a zookeeper.

CREATE YOUR OWN RULEBOOK FOR SUCCESS

1 Start by writing a new set of principles – ones that aren't affected by other people's views. Use the space below for your initial thoughts. Think of what you want to achieve, then work backwards charting the steps you need to complete in order to accomplish your aim. In some cases this is very important. For example, it would be tricky to become a marine biologist if you didn't get good grades in science.

2 Then begin thinking about any deadlines you might want to set yourself and note them below, like 'complete a beauty course by age 21', or 'volunteer at the local veterinary clinic by the time I'm 18'. You might be wondering why this helps. Deadlines give you a timeline to work towards, turning you from a dreamer into a doer. You don't have to stick to them (they're your own deadlines, after all) but you might find they help you visualise how you're going to make your dreams become a reality.

3 Get going. It's an exciting prospect once you start checking off your steps and get moving towards the life you really want. Just remember, you can be successful in tons of ways that don't include straight-A grades, driving a fancy car and living in a big house. As long as you're pushing yourself to be a good person with goals that make you feel happy and excited, you'll glow – because success is whatever you want it to be, it only takes a sprinkle of self-belief.

NO NEED FOR EXCUSES

There are real benefits to be gained from taking responsibility for everything you do

Have you ever blamed the dog for eating your homework or a sibling for kicking a ball through a window? Passing the blame often starts at an early age. Whether it's to escape the wrath of a teacher or a parent, it often seems easier to attribute your flaws and failings to someone or something else.

You're late for school, so you decide it's the bus driver's fault for getting stuck in traffic; you burn your toast, but snap at your sister for distracting you; you turn up soaked when meeting a friend and berate the weather. Some days, pointing the finger of blame in a particular direction seems the best way to deal with shortcomings. However, you could have left home 20 minutes earlier, kept an eye on the toaster and packed an umbrella. Is it time to accept accountability?

As prime minister Winston Churchill said when receiving his honorary degree at Harvard: 'The price of greatness is responsibility'. People who blame others for their mistakes learn less, lose respect and rarely achieve their potential. When you take ownership for slip-ups or oversights, success often follows.

HOW TO TAKE RESPONSIBILITY

Focus on learning
Everyone makes mistakes, it's all part of life, but not everyone has the courage to admit they were in the wrong. If you accept that you're responsible for your actions and that the reason you didn't get the grade you wanted was down to your lack of preparation rather than the exam board's poor questions, this proves you're adaptable and willing to learn and move on.

There's no need to punish yourself or feel that a failure highlights a character weakness or lack of ability. Instead, turn imperfections into opportunities. If you become more aware of possible consequences to actions, good and bad, then you'll make better judgments in the future. Accepting the blame demonstrates level-headedness and inner strength, traits that tend to earn respect.

Stay in control
The minute you place blame on someone else, you also pass them power. Without realising it, you're allowing them to take control of a situation – and, to a lesser extent, of you. This can make you more vulnerable and open to further criticism. Not taking responsibility may initially feel more comfortable and less demanding, but in the long run there could be a price to pay. If you accept the blame and appreciate that you could have acted differently, you hold onto the reins.

Know what's important
When you want to protect your pride, it's easy to blame someone else for a mistake, especially if they're not around to defend themselves: 'I didn't jam the printer, Emily from Year 10 was using it earlier.' But lying, or being economical with the truth, might make you feel guilty and this could gnaw away at you. Crossing your fingers and hoping no one will find out the facts won't accomplish anything. Own up and those guilty feelings will disappear.

Enjoy happier, healthier friendships

If you have a tendency to blame others for the slightest infraction, chances are you'll lose friends. Few people enjoy spending time in the company of a person who refuses to see their own flaws. It's understandable that people will give you a wide berth if you frequently criticise others – they'll be wary of what you might do or say about them. If you are accountable for your own behaviour, relationships can flourish. Being honest and open about being a normal person who makes mistakes helps to build stronger connections and improves your credibility. It bonds people together.

End negativity

If your default action is to unfairly accuse others whenever a problem arises, then it's probable that you're someone who sees the world in a negative light. Saying 'it wasn't me' becomes second nature, but it's unlikely to improve the situation. If you're unhappy with parts of your life, don't play the blame game. Instead, try to tune into your initiative, think positively and make changes. And if you're willing to accept responsibility when things go wrong, then surely it's acceptable to take the credit when all is well – and that's a great feeling.

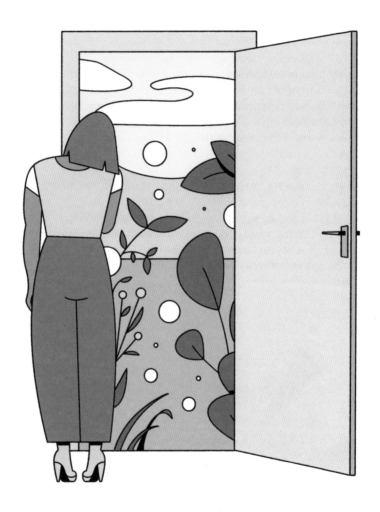

JUST SAY YES

Are you afraid to try something new? Many people stick to the things they are familiar with and avoid new challenges. After all, what if you fail? Or worse, make a fool of yourself? But there's a lot to be said for saying yes to opportunities. You may find you learn a skill, develop a hobby, make friends or even pave the way to your dream job...

Be brave

When you try new things, it increases your confidence and helps to build your self-esteem. Saying yes to one opportunity usually motivates you to say yes more often, opening your life to people and adventures. Courage and confidence are wonderful attributes to nurture. They inspire others and make you feel good. Even if you try something and you don't like it, at least you tried. After all, nothing you do is ever a waste of time. You can take something from everything – even failure.

Ditch the routine

Exploring the unfamiliar is a great way to shake up the daily routine and view life from a different perspective. Sometimes all it takes is one new experience to break bad habits and see everything more clearly. It's like having a little space to recharge and refocus and who knows it may even help you face the more challenging areas of your life. When you open up to challenges you have a greater sense of being present in the here and now. This means you're less likely to be thinking about the past or worrying about the future.

Make new friends

If you consider how you made your friends it was probably over a shared experience. Seeking out activities enables you to meet new people and make friends. People enrich your life and it's wonderful to learn and share experiences with others. Especially if you can motivate one another along the way.

Be happy

Probably the best thing about trying new things is you may find you enjoy them. Life is wonderful when you spend it doing the things you love with the people that lift you. So why not seek challenges and seize opportunities when they arise? Life should be full of happiness and trying new things is a great way to realise your potential and have some fun along the way.

Move on

Throughout your life, you may say no to something and later regret your decision. Missing opportunities can feel like you've let yourself down. You may also wish you had more courage and motivation to take yourself forward, especially if you see others thrive on an experience you had previously declined. But it's rarely too late to learn something new and it's wise not to dwell on a past decision. The best thing to do is learn from it and make a promise to say yes should an exciting opportunity arise again.

Go for growth

Saying yes to experiences helps you to live your life to the full. Opening your mind and enabling you to realise your full potential. Growing and developing also help to build confidence and while you're learning you're more likely to focus on the positives in life. When you step back to enjoy what you've accomplished and how far you've come you can feel an enormous sense of achievement. This can motivate you to keep going.

PRESSURE OFF

Do you constantly compare yourself to others and feel your achievements are falling short of theirs? Or do you often expect too much of yourself? These are common experiences. There are, though, ways you can shift your thinking to recognise how well you're doing in your own right, while pushing yourself towards your goals in a happy and healthy way...

Having people to look up to is immensely positive, whether you're acquainted with them in real life or not. They can provide inspiration for your own goals and achievements, as well as demonstrating how to attain them.

And of course, achieving a goal feels great, doesn't it? As with most things in life, however, there's sometimes a flipside to the greatness. Here, it's the pressure to maintain a standard. Scoring a high mark in a test might leave some people worried about performing similarly in the next one, for example, while gaining a reputation as the fastest runner or best chess player might create anxiety about living up to the hype. Have you ever had a teacher return a piece of work to you with the words 'not up to your usual standard' and felt somehow more crushed than if you'd received a lower grade on a subject you've never especially excelled in? Perhaps you've had a parent or carer say, 'I expected more of you.' Failure to meet expected levels of achievement or behaviour tends to feel worse when those levels are set high.

Standard issue

Sometimes, the image that someone is trying to live up to is an idealised version of themselves. Where does this image come from, though? It can be from others who have formed an impression of you, but it can also be a pressure that comes from within. Sometimes a person's expectations of themselves can be far higher than any expectation someone else has of them – a truth summed up by the saying 'We are our own worst critic'.

In other instances, it may feel like you have to reach the same standard as a person who has walked the path before you. You could have a teacher who previously taught an older sibling and you feel you need to be as good as them. Perhaps you've been made captain of a team or been assigned a role in a play that was previously held by someone else. In any of these instances, having a predecessor, the person who came before you, may create the feeling that there's a standard that needs to be lived up to – especially if someone tells you 'You've got big shoes to fill' or 'That's not how they would have done it'.

No one's perfect

So maybe it's not the way that someone before you would have done things, but that's not to say that they were right and you are wrong. Just as there can be many ways to reach the right solution in a maths question, there are often many ways of reaching certain desirable outcomes and, unlike a maths question with only one right answer, real life frequently offers more than one desirable outcome.

Looking up to someone who has trodden your path before you can be valuable, but at the same time, don't be afraid to recognise the fact that even a person you idolise cannot possibly be without faults – after all, no one's perfect. Learn and be inspired by the person whose standard you aspire to, but don't hesitate to critique them positively by looking at where you can improve on their actions or instigate brand new ones. The same applies to when it's your own past successes you're seeking to live up to: be proud of your efforts, regardless of what has been achieved by you or anyone else before.

You can't please everyone

No matter what you do, there's inevitably going to be someone who thinks it could have been better or even cases when it definitely could have been better. Criticism and less-than-perfects are a fact of life, so be prepared for them. In some instances you may want to take them on board and learn from them, while in others you may need to have a thick skin that enables you to shake it off and move on. Wanting the best from yourself is admirable but try not to focus too much on previous successes: this kind of thinking can be paralysing. Instead of thinking you have big shoes to fill or high bars to reach, aim to be your best and most authentic self on that day and in that situation. You are enough.

FORCE FOR GOOD

There are many anxiety-inducing stories about social media, which can make going online seem like a scary prospect. But let's not forget just how incredible the internet is and all the positive benefits it can bring. Here's a reminder of some of the many ways you can go online to enhance your life...

Connect with people
It's great to use social media to speak to mates you see all the time – but what's more amazing is connecting with friends and family who live far away and who you don't see often. You can use Facetime or Skype to speak to loved ones and take them on a guided tour of your home, let them join you on your holiday, show off your new haircut or wish them a happy birthday with a smile. In just a few seconds, you can connect with anyone around the world. Take time to get in contact with someone you've not spoken to in ages – you'll make their day.

Capture the moment
Using social media sites such as Instagram allows you to upload your favourite photographs and videos to one place and share them with friends and family. Having so many memories in one place is like having a visual diary. Make a point of looking back at them and remembering the cool and interesting times associated with them. It's amazing how quickly things and people change.

Express yourself
Do you have a skill or lots of ideas you think others would like to read about? If so, you can create your own blog to share your opinions on the world, or detail a project. It could be you create it via a site like wordpress.com, or create your own YouTube channel. Whatever you do, ask a guardian's permission in the first instance and then be careful not to reveal too much personal information. Safety first!

Raising awareness

If you're passionate about a particular cause or charity, look it up online or on Facebook and join a group – or you could even set up your own group to raise awareness. If you're over 16, you could set up a change.org petition and get friends and family to join your campaign for something you really believe in or that you think needs changing.

Learning new skills

Do you fancy yourself as the next guitar or turntable sensation? Or do you have the urge to throw some yoga shapes or brush up on your artistic skills? One of the many benefits of the internet is the access it provides to millions of YouTube tutorial videos and apps that can teach you a skill or develop a talent. Just search for the skill you want to acquire and you're bound to find something to help you. Watch out, world!

Educational benefits

When previous generations wanted homework or revision help, they had to head to the local library and take a book out. Today, it's possible to access millions of websites on every subject imaginable and find the answer to any question you have. You can buy books online and read them instantly or go to sites such as Fact Monster and Study Geek for extra help. There are also apps covering many school subjects and apps to organise your diary (though this will remove any excuses for handing in homework assignments late). You can also go online to check out colleges you're interested in or find out what you need to do for certain careers.

Getting support

What's particularly helpful for some is the ability to get support from others for problems they may feel uneasy talking about openly. For example, if you're struggling with something such as your health or feeling anxious or depressed, there are many sites that can help you with information and advice. There are also support sites such as Childline where you can share your problems with supportive people online anonymously from the privacy of your own home.

Fun times

One of the biggest developments in the last decade is the increasing number of films, TV shows, music and games available online. The arrival of the likes of Netflix, Amazon Prime and Apple TV has opened up the ability for people to watch back-to-back episodes of their favourite shows whenever they want if they pay a monthly fee. Downloading games, including hits such as *Fortnite*, has become huge, and many people listen to music online rather than buying it. One thing's for sure – if you have access to the internet, you'll never be bored.

THE POPULARITY STAKES

Why being number one in the cool gang isn't always as good as it might first appear to be

At any school, in any class, the popular kids are always easy to spot. Often it's something obvious, like wearing their hair a certain way, or carrying the latest bag or phone. Sometimes it's something less tangible – an attitude, a walk, the slang they use. Most people, at one time or another, have wished that they could be part of such a group. They may even try to change their behaviour or appearance to attract the approval of the popular kids. Something as simple as an approving comment from someone you admire in this way can put your head in a spin – imagine being invited to eat lunch with them or go to a party together.

Whether you're on the popular or less popular side of the fence, however, things aren't always as glossy as they seem...

Peer pressure

As much as it may appear that the in-crowd have it all, what many people fail to realise is that there's a flipside to popularity, too. For one thing, it's a slippery concept. In the same way that fashion is fickle and styles seem to go almost as rapidly as they appear, attitudes about someone's coolness can shift overnight.

Because of this, popular kids tend to be aware of the expectations of their peers, and expectations – any expectations – can often feel difficult to live up to. Striving to maintain a certain cool status can lead to pressure to participate in certain behaviours that are risky, or uncomfortable, letting grades drop, for example or talking back to teachers and parents. In some cases, the behaviours can be even more dangerous and involve experimenting in illegal activities.

Top-dog difficulties

Being popular may also mean certain responsibilities are imposed and not every popular person may feel up to what these involve. For example, someone who's perceived as alpha – the leader of the group – may be called upon to sort out problems and disagreements between other members of the group when actually, they'd prefer not to express an opinion. All eyes may turn to them when the question 'what should we do today?' is asked while they're secretly wishing that somebody else would come up with something for once. They might also find it difficult to carve out any time alone because they're constantly surrounded by friends or people who want to be their friends.

Adult opinions

Certain expectations of popularity may also be placed on kids by adults. Parents are sometimes the drivers of this, often because of the assumption that popular kids are happy kids or perhaps because they have their own memories of what it meant to be popular when they were younger. However well meaning parents are, this can put unwanted pressure on students, especially if their encouragement is along the lines of 'Why didn't you audition for the lead role in that play?'

Lonely at the top

Popularity doesn't always equal well-liked. For instance, some people are perceived as popular because they have a status – they might have secured the lead role in the school play, be head girl or captain of the football team. But, although they might be popular within their immediate circle, they might also be the object of envy and dislike from larger groups of people. For someone who's a genuinely decent person who wants to be liked, being the recipient of this negativity can be baffling and hurtful.

Do what makes you happy

Because popularity is measured by other people, popular kids might struggle to feel comfortable about their status. It's similar to how the number of likes on a social media post can affect someone's feelings about what they upload. Someone who's more passionate about a subject or cause rather than what others think of them and their interest can enjoy a sense of real freedom. Pursuing (and posting) what makes you happy and engaged is more fulfilling than trying to earn other students' approval.

You are unique

Ultimately, the measure of anyone's worth comes from within. Be the kind of person you would want to have as a friend and help others feel good about themselves, and you can hold your head up high. Kindness, respect and humour are qualities you can like in yourself and they make a person genuinely likeable. It doesn't mean they'll make you the most popular kid in school, but they will help you to look at people – even those popular kids – more compassionately.

THE ART OF ARGUMENTS

Disagreements are inevitable, even between the best of friends – but there's no need to fret or fall out. Instead, learn constructive ways to deal with your differences

From how much pocket money you should get to a friend's broken promises, there's always one topic or another up for debate. And while these passions can bond like-minded souls together, they also have the potential to rip relationships apart.

But disagreeing with a family member, friend or peer doesn't need to end in heartache. Exchanging views is constructive. During a discussion, alternative opinions can be shared, lessons in compromise learned, negotiation skills practised and when you make it through to the other side, you may even discover a newfound trust and respect for the person involved – and, of course, vice versa.

Difficult conversations happen every day and shouldn't be avoided through fear that an argument will ensue. Accept the reality that not everyone is going to see eye to eye. There will always be times when you'll disagree with someone you care for or they'll reject an idea of yours. But this is natural and it's healthy to have different opinions. Keep silent and you risk going down a slippery slope of negative emotion. When you feel strongly about a subject, but won't voice it, niggles can build up inside. This means you are suppressing your true thoughts and feelings, something that can create unnecessary tension and cause you to resent those around you. Be strong – you've every right to have your say. Debate the issue and clear the air. A battle doesn't need to commence, not when you take control and deal with a disagreement in these positive, effective ways...

43

DEALING WITH DISAGREEMENT

Focus on facts

During the conversation, try to concentrate on the facts – any evidence you've collected. Don't simply state a series of hypothetical 'what-ifs'. Of course it's important to be mindful of potential consequences of an outcome, but stay on the topic. Don't suddenly throw a curveball either, by bringing up a grudge that has nothing to do with the discussion. Okay, you're annoyed that a friend at school got chosen for Student Council instead of you, but if this subject is unrelated, avoid further confrontation.

Remain calm and composed

A disagreement doesn't need to be an argument. All you have is a conflicting opinion. There's no reason why you should get agitated or raise your voice. Stay calm, pinpoint what the main issue is and eloquently put over your viewpoint, stating why you want it heard and considered. Try to maintain the same tone of voice throughout any discussion, even if the other person appears to be shouting. You'll ultimately be seen as the one being more reasonable and respectful.

Learn to listen

You may be adamant that you're in the right, but listen carefully to what the other person is saying, and don't make presumptions. Only then will you be able to understand why they believe something is the right choice or course of action. Instead of devising another put-down in your mind, pay attention to what's being said. You may surprise yourself and hear ideas that make perfect sense.

Express yourself

It's all too easy to turn a disagreement into a personal attack, so be mindful of your language. Reflect and articulate how you see a situation, rather than criticising the other person involved. Instead of announcing: 'You never bother to spend one-on-one time with me', try a less accusatory option. 'I feel sad when we don't spend much time together', will encourage a parent to deal with your concerns rather than feel compelled to defend their actions. It's also more likely to get positive results.

Bite your tongue

Always think before you speak. A relationship can be ruined in the heat of the moment, so stop, count to 10 and don't allow spiteful words to spill out that will stun your 'opponent' in their tracks. There's no going back from hurtful comments, they can last a lifetime and are best avoided. The chances are you've only resorted to revealing an age-old resentment because you're feeling vulnerable. Being aggressive and causing hurt won't get you anywhere, though. You simply risk future disagreements.

Come to a conclusion

Always try to reach an agreement. Find any common ground, then together suggest ideas to bridge the gaps. Do your best to find closure that all parties are happy with – even if that's agreeing to disagree. But don't allow disagreements to linger. Remember, a difference of opinion is part and parcel of every healthy relationship. When you're next challenged, see it as a chance to learn and grow.

Celebrate your differences

Next time you get into an argument with someone close to you, it can help to remember that you are individuals with different ideas of what's important. Can you simply agree to disagree?

ONE FINE DAY

Everyone has times when they're feeling low and need a lift. One way to do this – and find some peace at the same time – is to bring to mind a favourite day and use visualisation (or mental imagery) to picture yourself back in that wonderful place and time

If you can, find somewhere quiet – a place where you won't be interrupted for at least 10 minutes. Close your eyes, take a few deep breaths and give yourself space just to be. Now, think back to a day that you loved and visualise it in your mind. See it from your perspective, as if it's actually happening again.

Bring in as much detail as possible. Really picture the day in your mind and be there – give it life and energy. If it was a day by the seaside, be yourself sitting on the shore with your fingers drawing lines in the sand or running into the sea, your body tensed awaiting the hit of the cold water.

Use all your senses to make the memory multi-dimensional. What did you see, hear, smell, taste and feel on the day? Place yourself back under a clear blue or cloudy, grey sky and in front of a turquoise or brown ocean – really see the colours. Feel the sun or chill on your arms – is there a slight breeze? Hear the waves wildly crashing or gently lapping on the shoreline. Taste the salt in the air or on a welcome bag of chips. It should feel as though you're really there.

Allow a smile to come to your face and your heart.

When you're ready, take one big, deep breath, open your eyes and continue your day.

MATTERS OF REPUTATION

How to avoid getting a bad rap and make sure you're seen in a positive light

Do you ever worry about what other people think of you? In life, people may try to define you in specific, often limiting, ways. Instead of focusing on this, it's important to shift your attention onto the opinions of close friends and family and being happy within yourself. Like it or not, however, you may still find yourself labelled – at school, in your community or at work.

A person's reputation is based on their actions and what others think of them. Few people talk about the idea of a 'good reputation' because most people tend to be seen in a positive light, but there'll always be someone who has a negative reputation – it might be for bullying, being argumentative, posting unpleasant pictures or messages online, or unruly behaviour in and out of school.

The thing is, in a world where many like to gossip, people can quickly change their opinions and it's easy to go from having a bad reputation to a good one – and vice versa. At some point, rumours tend to enter most people's lives and, while you can't do anything about them, there are ways to avoid being seen in a negative light.

STAND PROUD

Avoid gossip

Bad reputations can develop from hearsay and gossip. If you're friends with someone who eagerly tells you all about other friends' secrets and lives, it's likely that at some point they'll be talking about you in a way that might affect your reputation – and not always for the better. Don't forget, people love to create drama and most of the time rumours are exaggerated, so try to avoid getting drawn into idle gossip.

If you can, aim to judge people and situations for yourself rather than believing what's being said and consider how you'd feel if you were the one being gossiped about. It's also a good idea not to share your deepest secrets with the gossipers either. Always be careful who you trust with personal news or things you'd rather were kept quiet.

Friends matter

They say you can judge a person by the company they keep, so what kind of friends do you have? Your friends' reputations can easily rub off on you, so be wary about hanging out with people who are perceived in a negative way. You may choose to ignore what's said about them and make your own judgments, but if it turns out they're bullies (online or off), prepare to be labelled alongside them. That being said, if a friend suddenly gets a bad name for no obvious reason, you don't have to ditch them. Instead, defend and support them as you'd hope they would you. If, however, they've started behaving in a way that makes you feel uncomfortable, it may be time to reconsider your friendship.

Be honest

Lying and betraying a person's trust is a sure-fire way of developing a bad reputation. While it might sometimes seem the best option, lying rarely ends well and can prompt even close friends to consider how they feel about you. No matter how embarrassing something might be, it's better to 'fess up and face the music than lie and lose friends and your reputation. Everyone makes mistakes and people will value and respect your honesty.

Be careful what you post

Have you ever posted something on Instagram or Snapchat and regretted it immediately? Most people have at some point. The reality is, no matter how quickly you delete a selfie you come to regret or a spiteful post shared in the heat of the moment, someone out there will have seen it. Before you post, always pause for a moment and ask yourself: Is it kind? Is it inoffensive? Is it something I'd be happy for my family to see? If not, don't post.

Continue to be you

Consider what it is that makes someone have a good reputation. If others see you in a positive way, it's because you're friendly, kind, polite and helpful. Being seen in a good way is a reflection of how you treat others and, hopefully, that will be in a way you'd like people to behave towards you. Continue to be happy, kind and positive towards others as much as possible, even on your down days. No one's perfect and everyone makes mistakes but you can't get a bad reputation for being kind.

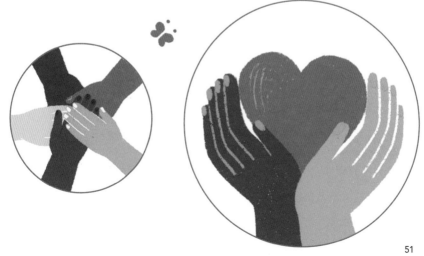

STEP INTO YOUR GREATNESS

A yoga pose that supports us in stepping forwards in our greatness and following our passions in life is Warrior Pose – *Virabhadrasana* in Sanskrit. It has three variations. Here, we explore the first, Warrior 1...

This pose strengthens the legs, opens the hips and chest and stretches the arms and legs. It also helps to develop strength, confidence, focus, balance and stability.

Here's how to get into the pose:

1. Stand tall, with your feet hip-distance apart and your arms dropping at your side. Take a few deep breaths here and feel the ground supporting you. Take time to connect with your core within.
2. On an out-breath, step your feet about 1 metre apart (to a point that's comfortable). Turn your left leg and foot out by 90 degrees. Turn the right foot in slightly, to about 40 degrees. The heels of the feet should be aligned with each other. Swing your hips around to face your left leg, bringing your torso to face the direction of the left leg. On an in-breath, lift your arms up over your head and stretch skywards with your palms facing each other. Take a few breaths.
3. On an out-breath, lower your tailbone (that's the bone at the bottom of your spine) towards the ground and bend your left knee into a deep lunge so that it is directly over your ankle and forms the shape of a right angle. Look up or forwards, lifting your upper torso upwards, while at the same time pushing downwards through your tailbone and legs.

Take a few deep breaths.

4. To come out of the pose, slowly straighten the left leg, turn both feet forwards, lower the arms and step back into standing pose. Take a moment to observe how you feel and then repeat the above for the opposite leg.

Always check with your doctor first if you have any medical or physical conditions that may be aggravated.

ONE WORD

Choosing a single word to guide you through life's challenges
can have a surprisingly big impact

On a shelf above my desk sits a box of beautifully designed alphabet cards. Each
card features a capital letter in a typeface reminiscent of early 20th-century
films. Every so often I take down the cards and use them to spell out a word.
At the moment my word of choice is 'respond'. Before I display the word on my
shelf I clear away all the surrounding clutter: staples, Post-it notes, pens, mugs.
This step is important because I need the word to have space to breathe and take
on an air of importance in the room. Once in position, the word becomes my
guiding light for the coming days and weeks.

Be inspired

The practice of choosing a word and allowing it to guide you is nothing new. I came across the idea a few years ago while browsing the blog of Ali Edwards (aliedwards.com) a designer, author and workshop instructor. In January 2006 Ali selected a word to focus on for 12 months while going about her daily life. The word she chose was 'play'.

'I thought a lot about play and what it means to me,' she writes. 'For me, it was a lot about living without fear – about being more open to experiences with an attitude of playfulness.' The exercise was so successful that Ali has spent the last decade repeating it with different words. So far they have included 'peace', 'nurture', 'vitality', 'open' and 'thrive'.

Part of Ali's tradition involves asking readers to send in their words, which she compiles into a master list – these make for fascinating reading. Who would have guessed, for example, that 'aroha' (the Maori word for love and affection) would ever appear, or that 'geek' could be an inspirational term? Most of the words, however, fall into one of two categories. They either describe things people would like to add to their lives, or things they would like to remove. The word 'peace', for example, makes a regular appearance, while the word 'fearless' is a popular choice.

Time to choose

So how do you choose a word? And what do you do with it? Well, sometimes the best course of action is to let a word choose you. Is there something you keep saying, or thinking, to yourself? Maybe you look around your room and feel overwhelmed by the amount of stuff you own. If so, why not pick a word that encourages you to take positive action – 'declutter' or 'simplify', for example? Better still choose a word that sums up how you would like to feel once your room is clutter free: 'calm', 'peaceful' or 'relaxed', for example. The most important thing is to choose a word that speaks to you and try not to be swayed by other people's opinions. The word you choose needs to make you feel excited, empowered and energised. You need to be in love with this word!

Let it be seen

Once you have settled on a word, make sure that it is somewhere that is visible to you every day. You could write it on a piece of paper and slip it into your diary or journal. But don't use any old scrap of paper – this is an important word – find a beautifully designed card or a vintage notelet and write your word with confidence and a flourish. The way you display your word is entirely up to you, however it does need to be visible, to act as a prompt. Once it is in position, read your word aloud every day. Turn it into a mantra.

Change it up

It's okay to change your word if you no longer find it helpful – don't be a slave to it. The word you have chosen might only be relevant to a specific project or certain period in your life. If so, let it go. But make a note of it all the same because looking through lists of previous word choices can tell you a great deal about who you are and who you hope to become. My previous words have included 'focus', 'calm', 'simple' and 'change'. Since I began the exercise a few years ago I have got rid of around 60 per cent of my clutter and moved to a new city. I'm still working on the calm aspect, but there's no rush.

Stop and think

You can let your word percolate, subtly influencing your actions, or you can use it more directly to assist you in decision-making. If you get a bit lost, stop what you're doing and ask yourself what you can do right now to honour your word. If you have chosen 'declutter', for instance, why not throw away all the old dried-up pens on your desk? Similarly, if your word is 'calm', take a couple of mindful breaths, no matter where you are or what you are doing. They may be small steps, but each one will carry you closer to your goal.

Make it personal

When I chose the word 'respond' it was to remind me that while I might not be able to change certain events in my life, I could choose the way I respond to them. I've used the word to help me when I have encountered challenges at work and I've used it to calm me down when I have felt impatient with my friends and family. Often it's not a specific action that causes us distress, more the way we react to it.

Focusing on one word can be powerful. It can provide focus, comfort and it can be liberating. It's just one little word, but it can have a huge impact.

GREAT EXPECTATIONS

Why the lead-up to a special event can be as thrilling as the day itself

Have you ever heard the phrase: 'Yesterday is history, tomorrow is a mystery, today is a gift?' It's basically saying that you can't do anything about the past because it's gone and you have no way of knowing what's going to happen in the future, so you should make the most of the present.

In some ways it makes sense but, of course, you can learn a lot from history and, even if you don't know exactly what's going to happen, it's a good idea to be prepared for the future. But there's something else you'd be missing out on if you took the above saying too literally – anticipation.

Supersize the feeling

Anticipation is the feeling you get when you're looking forward to something, and the thought of whatever that thing is makes you happy and excited. It could be that you're going to see your favourite band playing at a concert or a festival, or that you're going on holiday to a place where you know you'll have fun. Or perhaps it's your birthday soon and you're expecting some special presents.

In some ways, anticipation can be almost as enjoyable as the actual thing you're looking forward to. Look at the way that people start feeling festive weeks before the Christmas holidays. Some of them have put up their decorations and bought gifts by the end of November .

You might think that's too soon, but they'd probably say they're just supersizing their anticipation. And if you're having a difficult time for some reason, or just not feeling happy, it's nice to be able to think about something in the near future that will make you happy.

Anticipation anxiety

Perhaps you're reading this and thinking that sometimes when you're waiting for something to happen, you feel nervous about it rather than being happy and excited. It happens to everyone at some stage – there's even a term for it – 'anticipation anxiety'.

Still, however much you tell yourself it's silly to worry about the future because you can't possibly know how it's going to turn out, sometimes it's difficult not to let panicky thoughts take over your mind.

Take a fresh look

There are several ways of looking at this. For a start, have you ever spent weeks dreading something, then, after it was over, thought: 'That was fine. Why did I spend all that time worrying?' That suggests that people often blow up situations in their minds to make them much worse than they ever could be in reality.

Even if it does turn out to be awkward and you wouldn't want to repeat the experience, you can always learn from it and think about what you'd do differently next time. See if you can try to turn some of your anxious feelings about a future event into happier, more excited feelings. For example, if you started learning a new subject at school and had to join a different class, you might feel nervous if you didn't know anyone and didn't know much about the subject. That would be perfectly normal, but what if you tried to turn it around? Instead of worrying, think: 'I'm going to have the chance to learn new things and meet new people', which would be a different kind of anticipation.

Imagine you had to wait

Believe it or not, it wasn't always the case that you could watch your favourite TV show whenever you liked. Perhaps you're a fan of *Friends* – you can watch as many episodes as you like on Netflix. But back in the 1990s when it was first popular, viewers had to wait from week to week for new episodes. Imagine waiting for what seemed like forever to find out if Ross and Rachel would get together.

Now most people stream or download TV programmes, films, music and books in a second, without pausing to consider it. Why waste time hanging about when you can get something immediately?

It's a good point, but couldn't it also be the case that you appreciate things more when you've had to wait and think about why you're so desperate to see, listen to or read something? Or, at the very least, it means you have something to look forward to until then.

If you love *Star Wars*, for example, imagine if someone gave you a ticket for the latest movie that very afternoon. That would be a treat – but if they got you a ticket for the following weekend and you had to wait three or four days, you would have that nice feeling of knowing that something exciting is going to happen. That's the beauty of anticipation – you not only get to enjoy that something special, but you also get the added enjoyment of looking forward to it.

As the anticipation builds

Is looking forward to an event as exciting as the big day itself? Or is it nerve-racking or, maybe, just boring? Ask yourself these questions and explore what anticipation means to you:

*   What are you looking forward to right now?
*   How do you feel when you think about it?
*   What was the last thing you remember really looking forward to?
*   Did it live up to expectations? Or did you enjoy the 'looking forward' part more than the event itself?
*   Do you think it's a good idea to have things to look forward to? Why?

'YOU GET THAT FROM YOUR DAD'

If the way your family views you is holding you back, here's how you can rewrite the story and become the author of your own life

Have you ever been told 'you're just like your mum' or 'you get that from your dad' or 'you were like that even as a baby'? Family stories are often funny and full of love, but sometimes they can feel as if they don't reflect who you are as a person today. Your view of yourself starts to form from an early age and is heavily influenced by how others around you, including your family, see you and talk about you. Family stories that members tell about each other are particularly important and influence how people are perceived. The view of who you are and what you're like can be flexible, though, and change as you get older.

Everyone knows that feeling when your mum or dad repeats for the millionth time a story about how you or a sibling could never tell the time/tie your laces/ understand jokes. These stories can help add to a sense of belonging and are often loved and cherished memories. But what about when they keep you stuck instead?

Different person

Maybe as you get older you've changed your way of relating to people or altered something important about your appearance, and these family stories might make you feel that you can't move forward and be someone different. Perhaps when you were younger you had short hair and loved playing in the mud, but maybe now as you've got older you'd like to express a different side of yourself, while your family still see you in this earlier role.

Unfortunately, family members can sometimes be slow to see changes in personality and style and this might leave you feeling frustrated if you're not understood for the person you are now. At the extreme end, family stories about how you used to be could make you feel that your life path and chances are already set out for you.

What's so important about stories?

An approach called narrative therapy suggests that the stories people tell about themselves and others can have huge power over them. This approach suggests that these stories or narratives can shape a person's sense of identity, belonging and positive view of themselves. On the flipside, however, they also have the potential to provide an overly negative view of yourself that limits your self-esteem and might mean you miss out on the possibilities in your life. Luckily, there are always alternative stories to be told about a person or a situation, which offer freedom of opportunity and greater self-esteem.

Stuck in a role

It can be helpful to reflect on how certain family stories make you feel. Talk it through with a friend or make notes on your phone or in a diary. What is the initial emotion that you experience? Is it joy, happiness, frustration, anger or love? How does this story reflect who you are now? You can rate how accurate you feel it is now from 0-100 per cent and also how accurate it has been in the past.

Perhaps you're someone who used to be argumentative, like your dad or another family member, but you've become less so as you've got older and now happily discuss differences. Repeatedly being told that 'you're the one with the bad temper', however, is a sign that others haven't seen how you've changed and it might hold you back.

Rewriting your story

What are the positive things about you or family members that don't get told as much? If you could rewrite your story to feel more helpful and make you proud of the traits you've inherited from your relatives, what would you say?

Perhaps no one ever says your sense of humour is just like your grandad's, that your warmheartedness is really similar to your auntie's or how your stubborn streak (just like your mum's) is actually what gave you the persistence to win that sport tournament – maybe you can see that persistence in other people in your family too. Once you start looking for other connections and elements you might be surprised at what you find. If you go a step further and talk to your family about what you've noticed, you may find that they come up with new ideas also, either about you, your siblings or themselves.

It's possible to be thankful for family memories and stories and to respect those who cherish them. But don't forget that there's also room for you to make up your own mind as to whether these stories apply – and are helpful – in your own life.

Your story is your own. You're its author and you can decide if other people's contributions are welcome. Now, what's the next chapter you'd like to add?

NEW HABITS, NEW YOU

Make your return to school stress-free by planning for a fresh start and a new, improved and more positive you

After the long summer holiday, returning to school will evoke many feelings. Some of you will feel excited about seeing friends again every day, getting back into a routine and embarking on a new school year. Others will feel overwhelmed by the idea of normal life resuming or perhaps the looming exam pressure ahead. It's normal to feel a mix of emotions when you return to school, but with your mind and body relaxed and refreshed after your break, why not use this term as an opportunity for a fresh start and a new, improved you?

YOUR BEST SCHOOL YEAR YET

Reflect and plan

As the new school year approaches, spend time reflecting on last year and what went well for you and what you would like to improve. Then, make a list of the things you want to change, however unachievable some might seem. For example, it could be friendship issues, a certain lesson you want to improve on or doing something you think will make you a better student, such as completing all homework on time. It could be an aspect of your character you want to change, such as speaking up more in class, or it could be joining groups, like the student council.

Take action!

Once you've made a list of what you would like to change, select the aspects you will work on first. Choose ones that seem challenging but will be achievable with effort and determination. Then, plan how you will achieve them. What will you need to do it? Who can help you? What changes will you have to make? For example, if it's organising your homework better, it could be creating a homework timetable, going to a homework club or creating your own club with friends. It could also mean switching off devices at a certain time each night so you can focus properly.

New habits

However tricky making changes might seem at first, remember to be patient. If you persevere, even when things are difficult, the habits will become a part of your life and won't require as much effort as they seem to at first, especially when you start seeing the benefits. Even if you make a mistake or don't stick to your plan for a day or two, don't give up and think that's the end of your change. Instead, get back to your plan, knowing it will work out in the end. Look at any setbacks as challenges and remember why you wanted to achieve this in the first place.

New year, new style

To give the 'new you' a boost, treat yourself to something that makes you feel it's a real fresh start, such as beautiful stationery, clothes or an awesome haircut. You may want to tell others you are trying something new this year so they can support you, or you might prefer to write it in a diary, monitoring your progress and perhaps even rewarding any successes you achieve. You can also use your new diary to write down important dates and things to remember, such as homework, clubs or study sessions so you are super organised. Don't forget to book some relaxation time into your diary too!

Avoid drama for a happier you

Another way to ensure a happy school year is to ensure you are surrounded by people who you have fun with, who have a positive influence on your life and who will support your new habits. There will always be friendship dramas going on but if you found it was too much last year, resolve not to get involved this year. For some people, that may mean moving away from certain friendships that made you unhappy or learning to say 'no' if you feel uncomfortable about joining in with things. This can be daunting at first, but throughout your life, friends will come and go for one reason or another. Be open to new friendships and having a stress-free life.

New opportunities

One positive change you could make would be to make use of the extra-curricular opportunities available to you. School offers so many chances to learn new skills and develop talents and you never know, you may discover a hidden talent at a sport you never tried before. Either way, it's a good opportunity to make new friends and have fun. Find out from your school council, teachers or bulletin boards about what's going on. You don't have to commit to anything but by trying something new you might find it's one of the best decisions you ever made.

Banish the first-day blues

When you've been away from school for a few weeks, it can seem like a lifetime since you've seen some people and you might feel anxious as the first day back draws closer. It's natural to feel nervous about change or new starts but remember lots of other people will be feeling it too – they just hide it well! Luckily, most people find the nerves disappear when they're back in lessons, but if you're feeling anxious in the build-up, meet up with a few friends shortly before you return so you know there'll be some friendly faces waiting on that first day back. Whether you love or loathe school, remember it's just a stepping stone to the next stage in your life. Use your time there to be the best version of yourself, make the most of the opportunities on offer and enjoy the journey to achieving your dreams.

FLY WITHOUT FEAR

If the thought of soaring through the sky in an aeroplane makes you short of breath, don't sweat. There are things you can do to face your fear and see flying in a positive light

Holidays are exciting, but if you're scared of flying, the journey to and from your destination can cause a huge amount of anxiety. Maybe your belly flips when the plane takes off or you get the heebie jeebies when there's turbulence. Whatever sparks your fear, it's a horrible feeling to deal with.

And it's even worse when the rest of your family looks forward to a few hours above the clouds. In fact, it can be almost impossible to communicate just how frightening you find the whole experience when your mum is happily watching films, your brother is tucking into a stack of snacks and your dad keeps telling you to look out the window so he can teach you about the curvature of the Earth.

First things first: it's important to remember that you're not alone. Research carried out by *National Geographic* found that 20 to 30 per cent of people experience some level of anxiety when flying, from mild concern right through to full-blown fright. This fear is called aviophobia, or flying phobia. It's common and, it might be suggested, irrational because safety statistics say there is only a one in 11 million chance of something going wrong.

Anxiety, though, doesn't work like that – you can't just learn one fact and then switch off your terror. So, the next time you're set to get on a flight, try these calming techniques. They might not get rid of your fear, but they will help you manage your aeroplane panic.

Breathe deeply

It's common for nervous passengers to suddenly feel short of breath. Don't worry, it's a perfectly normal reaction if you're scared of flying. It happens because when your body is in panic mode, your breathing speeds up, sending a message to your brain that something is wrong. Calm that anxiety by controlling your breathing – slow it right down, in through your nose and out through your mouth. Continue to breathe deeply throughout the flight, especially when you feel your chest tighten (usually during turbulence). The benefits can be almost instant.

Distract yourself

This might sound impossible when your seatbelt is fastened tight and the plane is making weird noises, but try to occupy your mind with something else. Watch a film, listen to music, read a book, test your brain with a puzzle, draw, sketch or doodle. You could even try taking some homework on board. Anything to keep your mind from wandering back to those anxious thoughts.

Visualise the destination

Lots of phobia experts recommend trying a technique called visualisation. Basically, you imagine yourself stepping off the plane after the flight, safe and sound. It's crucial that you really envisage how it feels, how it smells, what you can see, hear and touch. Try to make the visualisation as detailed and as real as possible, and don't forget the most important part: the huge smile on your face.

Speak to the cabin crew

Cabin crew are trained to help and support fearful flyers, so pull one of the team aside at the start of your flight and share your concerns. Ask them to explain any unfamiliar noises, and to reassure you that everything is running smoothly during the flight, and remind you to keep using those distraction techniques.

Ask for extra help

If your fear of flying is really upsetting you, or stopping you from travelling, then ask your parents if it's possible to talk to an expert who specialises in fears and phobias. There are also lots of great courses that have been tailored to help you combat your fear of flying – check out your local airport for more info.

Don't forget!

Fear of flying is one of the most common phobias, so don't worry if the thought of being in the sky makes you feel sick, worried or anxious. There's plenty you can do to make yourself feel better, from simple breathing techniques through to a detailed distraction plan – and it'll be so worth it when you step off that plane.

RAIN, RAIN, GO AWAY

How to invite a little sunshine into your life when the skies are grey

Unexpected rainy days can be miserable, but unexpected free time can be a blessing. While the temptation might be to fall back on the same old habits – turning on the TV, catching up on chores, scrolling through Facebook – you can bring positivity into your day by trying something new. Here are some activities to help you make the most of being stuck indoors...

Meditate

Meditation can help you relax and be in the present moment, and allow you to, for a time, let go of your everyday anxieties. A rainy day indoors is the perfect opportunity to find some time to focus on yourself, let go of your worries and slow down your brain. Find a distraction-free, quiet space, sit on the floor with your back straight (sitting on a flat sofa cushion is perfect for this), set a timer (whether 10 minutes or an hour), listen to the rain pattering on the windows and concentrate on your breathing.

Start a mood journal

Journals are wonderful things no matter what you write in them. They record memories of a period in your life, and whether it's positive or negative, it can be cathartic and comforting to put your thoughts down on paper. An emotion journal is a great way to take hold of the present moment and freeze it – it can also help you track your moods, which could lead to you learning more about yourself and your emotional patterns.

Declutter your room

The KonMari method of tidying is a popular way to declutter your home, created by author Marie Kondo. The core of the KonMari method involves taking each item in your room and sincerely asking yourself whether it 'sparks joy'. The old jumper at the bottom of the wardrobe you never wear, the layers of clutter in drawers you never open – with KonMari, it's all gone. Remember to recycle what you can, or why not earn yourself some cash at the same time and set up a yard sale?

Pamper yourself

Taking the time to look after yourself can do wonders for your mood and happiness. Turn off your phone, run a bath and do whatever makes you feel most comfortable: add bath salts or play your favourite relaxing music. For even more revitalising vibes, try an exfoliating face mask to remove the dead skin cells on your face and leave you completely refreshed.

Drawing exercise

Walk around the room with a sketchbook and draw a portrait of the first face or animal you see. Can you give him or her a name? Or try some mindful drawing. Look around you and choose a random detail or object to observe. This could be something as simple as the grain on a wooden table. Look for others and sketch their patterns. How many different ones can you find?

Make your own recipe book

Collecting all of your favourite recipes into one place will show you how much you can do. You could illustrate them with coloured pens or images, and leave blank pages for those dream bakes you've not yet conquered, ready to motivate you to try them out. Writing out your own recipes means you can add all your personal tweaks and touches, too.

Cook from a different cuisine

Trying a recipe from a cuisine you've never explored will open you up to new flavours, techniques and ingredients you might never have tried before. For Japanese, you could try a tofu dish or the classic miso soup. For Greek, sample a lamb dish, such as kleftiko or a stew.

Write thank-you letters

Writing out letters of gratitude to the people in your life is an emotional and comforting exercise. Even if you don't actually mail them, taking the time to 'thank' the people in your life for what they do for you will remind you of the love and support that surrounds you, and if you do send them, your words and thoughtfulness will bring positivity to their day, too.

Create a scrapbook

Inspiration for scrapbooks can come from anywhere – you can use photos of you and your friends, create collages of places you want to travel to, or just use images and crafts to pay homage to your favourite colour palettes. You could dedicate a page to each of your favourite things – the beach, your dog, freshly baked cakes. Building a scrapbook is therapeutic, and there's no pressure to make it look a certain way. It's an expression of you!

Grab an umbrella and dance in the rain

And, finally, why not enjoy the rain itself? There's nothing wrong with a light shower, and a walk in the park with the fresh smell of rain can be rejuvenating and refreshing. Just make sure you wrap up warm when you get back inside!

INSTA-ANXIETY

Some posts can have a negative impact without the original poster even knowing it. Are you using social media positively?

Social media is a fantastic way to stay in touch with others and share information. One of the most popular ways to do this is via Instagram, which launched in 2010 as a photo-sharing platform. Now, though, you can use it for more than building a gigantic picture album as you can share videos, Instagram stories, create polls, exchange messages with other users and invite public questions.

Mostly, these are fun, but they can be used to cause upset by online bullies or those who think what they're writing is just 'banter'. Sometimes, the people doing this have no idea of the turmoil that results, which is why it's important to think about what you post to ensure social media is a positive experience for all – rather than a cause of anxiety.

Don't judge
An image may pop up in an Instagram story with the message 'Like for a rating', and this is one example of how social media can be negative. The poster is basically saying: 'Like this picture and I will judge you on a scale of one to 10'. Usually the rating is based on looks or personality or friendship, but it could be on anything – the poster can decide. Sometimes, the user will send the rating via a direct message (DM), but too often they will post a list of the likes on their page with their judgments or ratings next to them, showing everyone how they 'rate' other people. While this is fine if you get a good rating, it can be mortifying if the user judges you lower than everyone else.

If you're the one posting the 'Like for a rating', you might think it's fun – but consider how each comment or rating could affect the person, especially if it's someone you don't know well. Take into account the fact many people are unconfident about their looks. You may be a brutally honest person, but if you're not going to say anything positive, it's often better not to say anything.

If you're the one who receives a low rating, it will sting but try not to take it personally. This is just one person's judgment and perspective. Who are they to be the ultimate decision maker on who's attractive or what kind of person you are? It will hurt if they've done it publicly, but instead consider that the most important judge of you is you. And after that it's your real friends and family. In future, try not to get sucked into these polls. They rarely end well.

Sharing embarrassing videos

Another negative social media craze is filming others in embarrassing situations and posting the clips online. Often these are quickly liked and shared, causing humiliation for the subject, who may not have been aware they were being filmed. Sometimes, the film may have been set up – for example, tripping up a classmate or quietly pulling their chair away to get a reaction. Those behind the set-up and recording often claim it's just fun or banter, but it could also be considered bullying.

The embarrassment could have a profound impact on the person affected, denting their confidence and causing them a huge amount of stress and anxiety both now and in the future. If you see a video online and like or share it, you're contributing to the situation and it's almost as if you're supporting it. Instead, report the situation to a teacher or family member with the aim of getting the video removed and helping the student involved. Imagine how you'd feel if you were the one being filmed – what would you want to happen? You might think you'd find it funny, but you never know until it happens.

Direct attacks

When someone's angry with another person or just dislikes them, they can easily use social media to be hurtful. Whether it's tagging a student's name onto an insulting photo or writing cruel comments under their post, those with a vendetta can cause instant public humiliation and hurt. Another added feature of Instagram has been the ability to add polls to stories – while these can be used for quick questions, some use them as a means of attacking others, such as posting an image of a person and asking followers if they like them or think they're attractive. For the subject of the polls and posts, it can feel like the whole world is laughing at them – for them, this is cyberbullying.

HANG IN THERE

Failure is a hard thing to come to terms with. It can make you feel powerless and alone. And if it happens more than once, it's easy to think that you'll never be able to succeed and it might be better to give up altogether. Try to look at things differently. Success is within your grasp and overcoming obstacles is a talent that will help you develop as a person

Struggles are the essence of life

Can you imagine a life in which everything came easily? You wouldn't have to face life-changing decisions, stand up for what you believe in or even work hard to reach your goals. Wouldn't that be great?

The obvious answer may be 'yes', but it's not quite that simple: without goals and dreams to fight for, life's journey would be pretty boring and even a bit meaningless. Challenges can be a positive part of life and provide focus.

Tackling obstacles head-on tests capabilities and builds character. Challenges give you a sense of purpose, motivating you to succeed. They may test patience and self-belief along the way, but they allow you to appreciate what you have.

The tests you face today will also prepare you for the future. Try to accept them for what they are and see if you can change your attitude towards what some people think of as failure – they can be real learning experiences.

'Fall seven times, stand up eight.'

This powerful Japanese proverb says it all: life will knock you down more than once and it's up to you to get back up. It's really not about standing up the first time, but about persevering fall after fall. Keep getting up and moving on, no matter what life throws at you, and eventually you'll succeed.

It might be hard when you're in the middle of testing times, but try to be optimistic and don't be afraid of getting it wrong along the way.

Mistakes are an opportunity to learn and grow. If you fail, don't be defeated. Try again and try to identify where it went wrong last time. Look for an alternative route to reach your goal – maybe, as the proverb says, you'll make it the eighth time and it will all be worthwhile.

Any cause for celebration

Highlight your progress – not your disappointments. Recognise you're on the right track and appreciate each step forwards as a small victory that will get you even closer to your final goal. If you look at a mistake as feedback, rather than a setback, you can learn more from it. You can then use this knowledge to challenge yourself to find another way. It might mean stepping out of your comfort zone for a while, but you'll end up being proud of the courage you've shown. Most successful people have had to make sacrifices and overcome problems on their way to the top. Perseverance, passion, curiosity and imagination are all qualities that can help you push yourself beyond your own expectations. There are lots of famous people who could easily have given up before they made their mark.

JK Rowling, who wrote the *Harry Potter* books, was rejected by 12 publishers before one finally agreed to print her story. Those books went on to sell 450 million copies. If you surrender, you throw away your chance of success. If you keep trying and focus your efforts in the right direction, you can reach your full potential. You may falter, but make sure you also celebrate your successes, however small they seem.

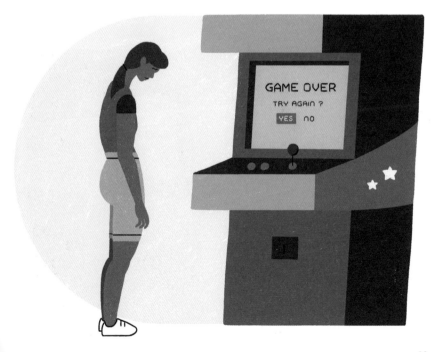

BRILLIANT MISTAKES

Five truly amazing unintentional inventions:

* **Tea bags**. When a merchant sent out samples of tea in pretty silk bags, people started dropping them straight into the water.
* **Penicillin**. Mould found growing in a dirty Petri dish led scientists to the discovery of antibiotics.
* **Post-it Notes**. When an inventor tried to create a super-strong adhesive, he accidentally developed a re-usable glue that made a great bookmark.
* **Silly Putty**. Attempts to design an alternative to rubber didn't go according to plan, but the result turned out to be a great toy.
* **The microwave oven**. A scientist working for a company making radar equipment noticed that microwaves had melted his chocolate bar, and used them to heat food.

BELIEVE IN YOUR DREAMS

Ambition can be a driving force for life. Believe in your dreams and have a good shot at fulfilling them. As the famous saying goes: 'If at first you don't succeed, try, try again'.

Perseverance is key
Once you've established a goal you truly want to achieve, keep going for it and be self-aware. Analyse each setback as it happens and identify any patterns. If the approach you're using isn't working, try a different one until you find a method or a strategy that works best for you.

Anything is possible… with planning and self-belief
Discovering a solution to the problems that are holding you back will make you see and believe that anything's possible. Devising a proper plan is essential, but also trust your instincts, especially if you're struggling to find answers.

Look at the bigger picture
If you hit a wall, don't give up. Think of a way around it, or under it, or over it. This may mean looking at the bigger picture and changing direction or adapting your goals. Re-thinking your route is a brave decision and certainly not a failure. It's another milestone on your journey.

Happy accidents
What if you look at the situation with fresh eyes? Stop focusing exclusively on finding solutions. Mistakes can also offer you new opportunities out of the blue, just by luck. If you are open-minded and ready to explore new ideas, you may find unexpected success… and by pure mistake.

GO AHEAD AND GIGGLE

Feeling down? All the more reason to have a really good
LOL now and then

What's the funniest joke you've heard recently? How about this gem:

'Why couldn't the bicycle stand up by itself? It was two tyred!'

Did that make you laugh, or only smile – or maybe groan? Whatever makes you
laugh, research keeps confirming there is some truth in the old saying 'laughter
is the best medicine'.

It's good for you

* Laughing releases endorphins, which help create the buzz that comes after exercise such as yoga, dance or running. Have you ever felt exhausted after a time when you have really laughed so much you nearly cried? That's because laughing uses muscles and it's that exertion that releases the endorphins, reducing stress. You breathe deeper to laugh, too, which means your lungs get a good workout as well.
* Laughter has been shown to reduce anxiety and calm stress hormones.
* A good giggle can give your immune system a boost.
* Research has shown that laughter may help to lower blood pressure – it's the reason therapies like Laughter Yoga have become popular.

Laughter connects us

'Laughter', the actor and comedian Victor Borge once said, 'is the shortest distance between two people'. Laughter crosses language barriers – you can share a laugh with someone regardless of your mother tongue partly because other people's laughter is so contagious. Laughter gives you a way of communicating together, and helps people to connect, groups to form and bonds to be made.

Just can't stop

Laughing at ordinary words, phrases or events is a common experience. Most people have giggled inappropriately at the back (sometimes at the front) of the class, at a serious moment, or (if you're honest) at a wedding, even a funeral. There's nothing more likely to keep you laughing than trying to stifle a fit of the giggles. Laughter is controlled by a part of your brain that evolved very early in humans' development as a species, alongside breathing and the control of basic reflexes. It's one of the reasons it's hard not to laugh even when you know you shouldn't. The laughter response is so deep in your brain that the more sophisticated parts of the brain, responsible for reasoning, logic and speech, have difficulty intervening.

Even so, uncontrollable laughter eventually stops. But in Tanganyika (now Tanzania) in 1962, contagious laughter that started among a very small group of 12- to 18-year-old female students rapidly spread to neighbouring communities. It reached such high levels that entire schools were closed. This bizarre epidemic lasted for six months. This is now considered an example of mass hysteria. Symptoms also included crying and flatulence.

It's a challenge not to at least smile at that last word. Some words, hysterically funny when you're younger, remain so your whole life. What else makes you LOL? Researchers have found that most laughter occurs during ordinary conversations rather than when you're listening to or telling a story or joke. The misheard quote, the unfortunate phrase, the 'trigger' words are some of the things that spark most laughter. You probably know someone (it may even be you) for whom the words 'squirrel' say, or 'moist flesh' are, in any context, hilarious – for reasons everyone may now have forgotten but which always sets you off laughing as well.

HOW TO GET MORE LAUGHTER IN YOUR LIFE

* When you're on your own, you're more likely to laugh if you watch, listen to or read something that's funny. So on those occasions, find your favourite show, online moment or book – make yourself comfortable, and settle in to laugh.
* Enjoy something funny with other people. Go to see a humorous film together or to a comedy club performance. Laughing along with other audience members can be great fun.
* Spend time with the people who always seem to end up making you laugh.
* Go to a Laughter Yoga club – or, if you'd rather, join in with one of the many Laughter Yoga videos on YouTube.

Researching this article has been a joy – and a source of much laughter. How fantastic to have to watch yet another YouTube video of cats falling off tables, or feel obliged to look up the funniest jokes. A waste of time? Not at all, not if it means you're laughing. It's just what the doctor ordered.

'ANYTHING'S POSSIBLE'

Being different, or looking different, can sometimes feel isolating or restricting. But with self-belief and the right support, everyone can achieve their own personal successes

Have you ever felt isolated or self-conscious because you looked different or felt out of place? Perhaps you got new glasses, joined a new school or started wearing braces. Human beings want to belong, but each individual is a unique combination of genes and experiences and differences are both inevitable and wonderful. Some people, of course, enjoy standing out from the crowd and wear striking clothes or have colourful hairstyles to make sure they do just that, while others prefer to blend in. For some, there isn't a choice. If you have a prosthetic limb, use a wheelchair or have scars, for instance, it can sharpen those feelings of being different.

Georgia, 20, is a confident, intelligent and positive university student. She also uses a wheelchair. Georgia was born with cerebral palsy, a lifelong condition

that affects movement and coordination. This means it takes twice as long and double the effort of most people to perform everyday activities such as showering, getting dressed and cooking. The condition – and the extra energy it requires for these tasks – is tiring, both physically and mentally.

Georgia is studying Special Educational Needs and Inclusion Studies at Canterbury Christ Church University in Kent, and hopes to become a speech-and-language or play therapist when she graduates. She admits, however, that the decision to move away from home to study was a daunting one. It's also been a big wrench for her mum, with whom she's very close. Even so, she encourages anyone who's disabled to go to university, adding that she's received lots of support in her studies and from other students.

In her school days, though, some pupils would sometimes stare at her or make unkind comments. 'Sometimes I was brave enough to explain why I'm in a wheelchair,' says Georgia. 'I think it's just a lack of education and understanding. I was fortunate that my friends were supportive and encouraging.'

Describing herself as a 'loud mouth', Georgia says she owes her positive mental attitude to her parents and a wheelchair skills club run by the charity Whizz-Kidz. The sessions include games like dodgeball and cookery as well as practical skills like navigating doors, scaling ramps, braking safely and picking things up off the floor. Whizz-Kidz gave Georgia an adapted trike, which developed her strength and stamina. It also flexed her confidence muscles. She says: 'I felt comfortable there because other people were in wheelchairs too. It became a big part of my week. Now I'm an ambassador and help other young people to determine how the service is run. I get a lot out of helping Whizz-Kidz.'

Through the charity, Georgia took part in the London mini-marathon and Westminster Mile wheelchair races – something she's keen to get back to once she's graduated. She said: 'I've met a lot of incredible people through wheelchair racing. It's also helped my confidence and people skills because I had to tell the organisers, coaches and other athletes if I felt something wasn't right. If you don't have confidence in yourself then how are people going to have confidence in you? I believe that anything is possible.'

Be different
Support people who have different needs. Georgia advises: 'If you see somebody in the street who is disabled, don't be afraid to have a conversation with them. Most of the time we're happy to answer.'

Don't presume, however, that you know what any other person wants. 'I've had my wheelchair pushed for me when I'm happy to do it myself,' explains Georgia. 'It's like somebody taking your hand and walking you down the street. We prefer it if somebody asks before they help us.'

Georgia admires comedians Jack Carroll, who was runner-up in *Britain's Got Talent* in 2013, and Lee Ridley, aka Lost Voice Guy, who both have cerebral palsy. 'They both have similar conditions to me but they haven't let it stop them from doing what they enjoy and making people laugh,' she says. Georgia's also pleased to see that toy manufacturer Mattel has created new Barbie dolls, one of which uses a wheelchair and another that has a prosthetic limb, and that there's now a *Sesame Street* character who has autism. She feels that these developments help to show all children that disabled people can do many different things at many levels.

Paralympian Lauren Steadman would agree. She was born without her lower right arm and says people's perceptions of her disability changed after she appeared on the BBC's *Strictly Come Dancing*.

She told the BBC: 'Before, kids and adults would look at me and see my arm first before they saw me. Whereas now they don't even see my arm – it's been normalised... I think that's how it should be, and it's just really lovely to be able to inspire everyone and show them that anything's possible.

FIND THE BRIGHT SIDE

If you've found yourself struggling with feeling different, here are a few constructive things you can do – and always remember you're not alone:

Talk to someone you trust. If you're feeling low, have specific things with which you need help or if you're being bullied, try to open up to your parents, guardians or family members you like and get on with and who will be able to arrange help. Friends who really know you and you trust will also help to boost your confidence and help to make you feel less isolated.

Find your tribe. There will be other people whose abilities are very like your own – some might be high-profile names in entertainment, business, science or the arts. Search online for places and organisations that are accessible to you or offer support and skills development. If you're not sure where to look, ask for help.

Follow your dreams. Ignore what other people might think – even if that's scary. As the title of the best-selling self-help book by Susan Jeffers advises, *Feel The Fear And Do It Anyway.*

FROM COUCH TO SUCCESS

How to get from procrastination to motivation

It reels you in with the promise of spare time to spend on the sofa, with friends or in virtual worlds but fails to warn you of the cloud of guilt and worry that will hover over any activities you choose to indulge in within this forbidden space. For while the procrastinator borrows time, it comes with a price.

What is procrastination?

Can you think of a time when you didn't feel motivated to study or work? When you felt tempted to put a task off until later, perhaps because it was boring, or a bit tricky? That was you procrastinating. The problem with procrastination is that it can leave you with an uneasy feeling, and this can get worse and worse until you eventually tackle the task. Getting the task done early, before the uneasy feeling kicks in, is a simple way to solve this, but many people find this difficult.

Why do I procrastinate?

The teenage brain is wired differently to that of an adult. The prefrontal cortex, the part that helps people think about the consequences of their actions, often doesn't fully develop until the mid-20s. This means it's harder to ignore the temptations of instant gratification. The positive feelings that come with successfully completing a task can feel far away in comparison to the immediate hit of doing whatever it is you're enjoying right at that moment.

To begin with, the instant hit continues to make you feel good, even with the light cloud of guilt and worry. But as deadlines loom the cloud gets heavier and, finally, panic shifts you into action. The task may well get done – you may even do a good job – but the chances are you won't enjoy it. This suggests to your brain that pressure and stress are necessary for success, and before you know it you're stuck in a cycle of procrastination.

How can I break the habit?

Think about a time when you completed a task and were able to lounge on that sofa without a care in the world. Remember how delicious that feeling of well-earned leisure time felt? Completing jobs can feel fantastic. By effectively planning and breaking larger tasks into small, easily achievable chunks, you'll reap the rewards of guilt-free leisure time. But, you probably know this...

So, why don't I already do it?

There are two types of motivation: 'away from' (something you don't want) and 'towards' (something you do want). 'Away from' motivation can provide a powerful kick-start but the situation needs to be pretty bad before it kicks in. 'Towards' motivation, in contrast, works by focusing on a clear and positive goal and, just like setting satnav, no matter how many times you take a wrong turn, it will recalibrate until you're back on track. In cases of procrastination, neither your 'away from' nor your 'towards' motivation are strong enough to compel you, so more immediate amusements win out, despite the light cloud overhead.

HOW CAN I INCREASE MY MOTIVATION?

1 Think about a task you've been putting off for a while, whether it's a school project or household chore.

2 Close your eyes and imagine you're walking along a road. Suddenly the road divides and there are two paths ahead of you.

3 Down the first path is a future where you continue to procrastinate. In your mind's eye, look down this route. What could the consequences be for you? What opportunities might you miss? Picture your worst-case scenario.

4 Step into the picture, allowing yourself to experience those uncomfortable feelings. Notice that you can play with this scene, adjust the brightness, the sharpness, the volume and intensify the feelings. Remember that your goal is to strengthen your 'away from' motivation.

5 From this point in the future, imagine looking back and seeing all of the unpleasant feelings that procrastinating has brought you. Experience the heavy cloud of guilt and worry.

6 Now, step out of that scene and come back to the present. Look down the other path, to a different future, one where you plan and work steadily on the task. Imagine seeing yourself having completed the task. What are you doing? How has completing the task benefited you? Picture your best-case scenario.

7 Now imagine the same moment but this time seeing it through your own eyes. What would you see, hear and feel at that moment in time?

8 Play with this scene, adjust the brightness, the sharpness, the volume and intensify the feelings. Remember that you want to create an irresistible vision to motivate you.

9 From this point in the future, imagine you could look back all the way to the present moment and see the individual steps you took to get here. This will help you to make a plan later.

10 When you open your eyes, do something straight away while it's still fresh in your mind. It doesn't matter how small. It could be as simple as gathering the materials you need to begin your project.

Celebrate! Make sure you reward that part of you that craves gratification. This will help to retrain your brain to recognise that completing tasks can be positive.

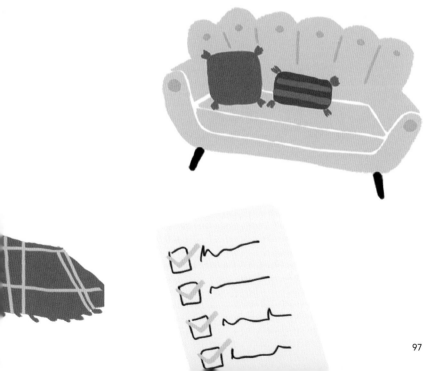

FIND YOUR FRIENDLY VOICE

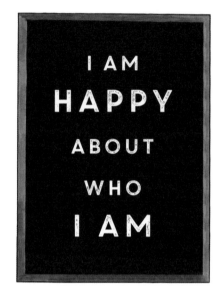

Why it's important to talk to yourself kindly, as you would a friend

Do you sometimes tell yourself things like 'I'm so useless', 'I'll never be good at maths' or 'everyone's way more attractive than me'? If the answer's 'yes', don't worry, you're not alone. Everyone has an inner voice and, unfortunately, it's not always the most supportive – in fact, sometimes it seems like it's never on your side. Luckily, there are ways to quieten it down and change your self-talk for the better.

What is self-talk?
You might not always be aware of it but your self-talk is the way you speak to yourself. It is your rarely silent, but often persuasive, inner voice. The one that constantly runs in your mind and affects the way you look at yourself and think about the world around you.

How inner chatter affects you

Self-talk can affect the decisions you make and influence how happy and successful you are on life's travels. If your inner voice is mostly positive, upbeat and encouraging, it will support you in how you feel and in the actions you take on a daily basis. For example, many top athletes and businesspeople focus on improving their self-talk to develop a strong resolve, which makes them feel more motivated to succeed, and be the best they can be.

If, however, it's always picking fault, and saying, 'I'm not good enough', 'I can't do that', 'I'm a failure' or 'I'm stupid, lazy, slow, ugly, useless, clumsy... ', then you might come to believe it – even though it's not true.

Self-talk can have an impact on everything you think and do, and keep negative thoughts in your mind. It might mean that you limit the challenges you accept, turn down chances you're offered and even put you off doing things you love. In many ways, this inner critic can stop you from achieving your full potential – if you allow it to.

Why is self-talk so negative?

Thoughts and feelings are complex and the sometimes negative, critical and incorrect script that goes on in your head can arise from how you've responded to various events and experiences in your life. It might be that a teacher gave you some feedback that included an area that needed improvement, and your inner voice has chosen to focus on this, and push to the side all the strengths that were mentioned. The result is you lose faith in yourself. Or it might be that you made a mistake one time and a group of nearby students started giggling. Your self-talk might feed on that and tell you how silly or clumsy you are, persuading you not to try again.

In some ways, your inner-voice is running in comfort or survival mode. It's trying to keep you safe so that you don't experience life's physical and emotional pains – it thinks it's protecting you.

'BELIEVE YOU CAN AND YOU'RE HALFWAY THERE'

Theodore Roosevelt

So, I make mistakes – it's part of what makes me human

THERE'S NO NEED FOR ME TO COMPARE MYSELF TO OTHERS

How to quieten the negative voice

The first step is to become aware of what it's saying. Be mindful. Tune into your self-talk and take note whenever you find yourself thinking something negative or self-critical. Perhaps you hear it saying you'll never be able to achieve something because you're not bright enough. Challenge that thought. Once you start catching negative self-talk, you can make a decision in that moment to quieten it and choose kinder, more supportive words and phrases that make you feel good about yourself and the world around you.

Choose positive self-talk

Once you're conscious of your inner monologue, you can change what it's saying. Think of self-talk as computer code that you can programme. That way you can re-code negative chatter with uplifting messages of encouragement that give you the courage to enjoy life's opportunities. To make positive self-talk your default mode so that your inner dialogue is like a supportive best friend, try to consciously repeat positive messages, often called affirmations, every day. You can do this at any time of the day or night, and either say them out loud or in your mind.

Why not give the positive affirmations on these pages a try?

HOME OR AWAY?

Some people revel in the prospect of sleepovers and school trips while others find them nerve-racking and would do anything to avoid them. If you're in the second group, you're not alone, but there are ways to make your feelings more positive...

The excitement of going to a party or starting at a new school can understandably be mixed with apprehension. For some people, however, the anticipation brings only fear – there's no sense of enjoyment at all.

Such feelings are difficult to handle within yourself and can also affect peer-group situations. Knowing everyone else is having regular sleepovers can make you feel isolated while class excitement about a school trip that you're dreading, or even choosing to miss, may heighten worries about what others think of you.

Home sweet home

Firstly, it's super important to know that nothing is wrong with you. It's not uncommon to occasionally, or even regularly, have anxiety about being away from home. You're not alone in craving the security of your own home, nor in fearing being away from it. Anxiety often stems from not feeling in control, so if you have a trip coming up, it might help to sort out your own bag and pack familiar items. Think about things you find comforting or helpful. Here are a few you could include:

* A cuddly toy.
* Your own toothpaste (you may not like the brand at your friend's house).
* Cosy pyjamas that you feel comfortable in.
* Your own pillow.

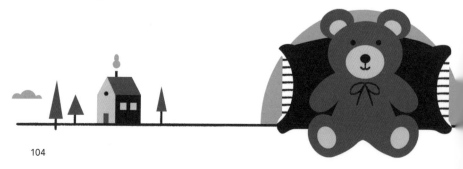

WAYS TO COPE

Blocks of time

Try working up to sleeping at a friend's house slowly, staying a bit later each time you visit. This familiarises you with their routines, making the differences between your home and theirs feel less overwhelming. You could stay until just before the evening meal at first, then until just afterwards, then until bedtime. It can also help to find out about things like the bathroom, where you will sleep and what time the lights will go out. Mental preparation like this can lessen those panicky feelings.

Breaking a situation down works in another way as well. Clinical psychologist Rachel Andrew says that giving yourself a 'lifeline' can make situations more manageable. For example, rather than focusing on the whole five nights at camp, concentrate on tonight and tell yourself: 'If I still feel like this tomorrow, I will ask to call home.' Tomorrow, you'll likely feel more in control, so extend the target to that evening. Then do the same until you're heading home anyway.

Parents are learning too

Getting things off your chest can alleviate your worries, so talk to your parents. They can also tell your teachers or friends' parents that they don't mind being called at any stage to collect you if things get too much. Remember, though, that watching their children gain independence often makes parents feel uneasy themselves. They may even seem confused or upset about your anxieties. Picking up on their emotions can make you feel worse, but parents miss having their children at home just as much as children miss being there, so try not to let their feelings heighten your own.

Communication

Confiding in friends can be useful and strengthens
relationships. It's also likely that some friends might have
similar feelings. Opening up to a group about being nervous can feel intimidating,
so you could try using general statements, such as: 'I've no idea what this camping
trip's going to be like, especially the bathrooms', and then wait for everyone's
responses. The chances are at least one or two will say there are aspects of the trip
that they're also worried about.

Coping mechanisms

Anxiety often manifests itself in real physical symptoms, like feeling sick, hot
or achy. 'Your body is trying to help you: think about it in this context so the
symptoms don't seem so overwhelming,' says Rachel. 'Concentrate on your
breathing, splash your face with water. Try picturing somewhere you feel safe
and calm.' Additionally, says clinical psychologist Angharad Rudkin, allow yourself
five minutes of 'worry time' and then distract yourself with thinking challenges,
such as naming all the players in your favourite football or netball team.

> 'THE MAGIC THING ABOUT HOME IS THAT IT FEELS GOOD TO LEAVE, AND IT FEELS EVEN BETTER TO COME BACK'
>
> **Wendy Wunder**

Decisions, decisions

You may not always feel the way you do now. 'For most people, home is where they feel safest, so being away can feel unsettling, which is completely normal,' says Angharad. It's also understandable if these fears make it difficult for you to make a decision about whether to attend an event or not. 'Psychologists call the build-up to a big event "anticipatory anxiety",' she explains. 'Beforehand, it's normal to feel anxious, with our heads full of "what ifs". Accepting this as a phase to get through will help you to not get too caught up in those feelings.'

It's also normal for all those 'what ifs' to paralyse your decision making, but, says Rachel, the more you make your own decisions – whether to go, or not go, whether to leave or stay – the more confident in your instincts you'll become, and the more empowered you'll feel about future situations. Don't beat yourself up for deciding 'no'. It's still your decision, even if it was made in a panicked situation.

Remember, too, that some people are naturally more outgoing than others. You may be someone who enjoys being alone and in their own space and, as long as it's not causing you to feel any anxiety or worry, then there's absolutely nothing wrong with that.

BEAT THE SUNDAY-NIGHT BLUES

Transform your thinking to give yourself a stress-free weekend

Picture the scene: it's a Sunday afternoon and you're having a fantastic time relaxing with your friends, watching your favourite TV show, reading an exciting new book, or doing something you love. But, suddenly, the sun sets and you know it's that time again – Sunday evening, which for you always means one thing, Sunday-night blues.

If you have a tendency to suffer from anxiety, you're certainly not alone as it affects many people. It's a harsh contrast to that fantastic Friday feeling experienced just two days earlier and often it disappears as soon as you go into school on Monday. If this sounds like you and it happens on a regular basis, it's time to work on ways to combat that anxiety so your weekends are more enjoyable. With just a few tweaks, you can beat those blues and the weekend will seem longer and lovelier.

What is Sunday-night anxiety?

Many people experience anxiety, but some only feel it on a Sunday evening, and the level will vary from person to person. For some, it will be a nervous sensation of butterflies in the stomach. Others might become suddenly irritable and moody, have difficulty sleeping or have a sense of impending doom and thoughts that race off in every direction. Unfortunately, it cuts that relaxing weekend short as the person can't stop the nervous feeling and imagining bad things that might happen on Monday.

Break the habit

Sunday-night blues can develop over time – they're anticipated, so they happen. Try to break the cycle by changing your routine. Do something different this Sunday, practise some yoga, go to see friends or head to the cinema. Anything that will throw your mind into thinking this isn't a normal Sunday. Instead of thinking of things that could go wrong on the Monday, try to change your mindset to visualise yourself having a good day, and things going right instead. Imagine the day as relaxing, happy and fun and it will take the edge off the worrying. Remind yourself that you have felt this way before and Monday is always fine. It's just a part of your brain (science bit coming up in next paragraph) making you feel this way and you can overpower those thoughts by focusing on positive things.

Sunday science

Some scientists believe that a part of the brain – the neocortex – is to blame. The neocortex works ahead of the in-the-moment thoughts and is already looking ahead to the next day. This can cause this feeling of dread and anxiety because the brain is thinking about going back into an environment that may be stressful or boring for one reason or another – or certainly not as relaxing as the lie-ins and chill-out time it gets at the weekend. Interestingly, that euphoric Friday feeling happens for the same reasons – the neocortex knows there's a relaxing Saturday ahead.

Write it down

Try writing down your thoughts about why you're anxious. Can a friend, teacher or another adult help you solve an academic or friendship issue? It is worth making a diary of the things that worry you and then, after Monday's been and gone, write again about how your day went so you can look back and see that often your fears don't come true. Write yourself a message for the following Sunday to remind yourself of what actually happened rather than what you feared might happen. Lots of people experience Sunday-night anxiety, but try to break the cycle and earn yourself a few more happy hours – you deserve it.

FINISH THE WEEKEND WITH A FLOURISH

Create a list of the ways you can make your Sunday a fun-day instead of stressful. Here are a few ideas to help:

* Organise your time so you don't leave homework or chores until the last minute.
* Get some exercise. A walk or gentle yoga practice can help to burn off any nervous adrenaline and might mean you find it easier to get to sleep, too.
* Call a friend and chat about any worries. If it's a friend you'll be seeing the next day, the chat could also give you something to look forward to.
* Avoid social media (or at least limit it), which can be distracting and cause anxiety if you see others' stories of amazing weekends. Some posts might even upset you so the worry carries through to Monday.
* Take a relaxing bath and read a book. This can give the brain a different focus.
* Try to plan trips and events to keep your mind busy, whether it's seeing a film, a hot chocolate with friends or even a box-set marathon.

Remember to have fun – it is, after all, what the weekends are for!

HOME DATES

It can be emotionally tough when your parents find new love, but there is a positive way through

Up. Down. Turnaround. Life has an annoying habit of turning everything on its head and bringing unwelcome change your way. Take your home situation. Even though your parents separated a while ago, it might be only recently that they've stopped quarrelling, things have settled down and a routine's been set up that suits all. But what if your parents have started dating new people, and now there's more emotional upheaval?

What if...?
Added to the stress of having to get along with their new partners, and the fact you may now have less time with your parents, your head is spinning with a million what ifs. What if your dad moves in with his new partner or your mum asks hers to live with you? What if their new partners don't want you? What if their new partner has children and they annoy you? What if one of your parents decides to have more kids? But do you know something else about what ifs? What if they never happen? And what if it all turns out fine?

Your reactions are natural
When a parent or guardian meets someone new, you may feel confused, threatened, sidelined, resentful and even guilty – you know your parents deserve to be happy, and deep down you want them to be, but part of you might be hoping their relationship won't last.

You may also be shocked or embarrassed by your parents' behaviour, if, say, they start acting like lovestruck teenagers, always texting their new partner, giggling at silly messages, or even making out in front of you. If that's how you're feeling, rest assured that your responses are entirely normal. Most people (of any age) in a similar situation – one that pulls them out of their comfort zone – will experience many or all of the same emotions.

Yet it's important to step back and to view things from a fresh perspective. Unless you have an actual reason to dislike this new person*, it can be better in the long run to try to find ways to accept them.

FIND THE POSITIVES

They deserve to be loved
Your parents have a right to fall in love with anyone they choose. If you've got a problem with that person, ask yourself why. Try not to look for reasons to dislike them. Just because they're taking up some of your mum or dad's time it doesn't make them a bad person. Conversely, if you do like them, don't think you're being disloyal to your own mum or dad. Granted, one parent may feel bitter if the other has found love when they haven't, but their desire for you to be happy will override that. In the end, they will be relieved that the new person is kind to you.

Explain how you're feeling
In the early days of a relationship, when people are falling in love, they often have eyes only for each other. If you think you're being sidelined, or that you're getting in the way, or are embarrassed by their shows of affection, speak to your parent about your feelings. Plan what you want to say first so that you can put your point across calmly. Remember that just because they have feelings for someone new, doesn't mean they love you less.

Set boundaries
If you see one of your parents for a limited amount of time, only at weekends for example, explain that you need some time alone with them (if that's how you feel). Say that while you're happy to meet their new partner on alternate weekends, you'd really appreciate it if they didn't come along to every meeting.

Avoid criticism
Try not to complain about your mum or dad's new partner to your other parent unless you have good cause to do so. It might create tension and make for an uneasy situation.

Get another's perspective
Talking to friends who are going through something similar can help, but try not to let it turn into one long moan. It might help to involve someone who'll tell you if you're being unfair or biased in any way.

Be patient

Give your relationship with the new partner time to develop. You don't have to like them, but being polite won't do any harm. Learning to get on with people you don't necessarily like is something that's likely to continue through life.

Look on the bright side

Your parents' new partners may have children already, and if the relationship continues you'll doubtless have to meet them. This added dimension will expose you to new circumstances and different dynamics that have to be negotiated.

If you find yourself struggling, or a parent or guardian's new partner makes you feel uncomfortable by saying or doing something inappropriate, talk to a trusted adult – an older relative, teacher, school counsellor or nurse will be able to help. Advice is also available 24 hours a day from Childline – childline.org.uk.

FRIENDS FOREVER

Creating a friendship book is a great way to celebrate someone special and it's a gift that can be treasured for many years to come

The word memento means 'an object that you keep to remember a person, place or event' and it comes from the Latin word for 'to remember'. Have you ever seen adults having a clear-out of old boxes, and then spending hours looking through all the photos, reminiscing and reading the letters that they've uncovered in the process? You can be sure that not much actually gets thrown out when this happens. A trip down memory lane is a lovely way to pass the time, but although our minds hold all of those memories somewhere in their depths, tangible things can bring them to the fore and make them more vivid.

The memories that friends build over time are precious. Even as you get older, that shared history is like a glue in your relationship, so giving that history a physical form by way of a friendship book is a gift that your BFF is sure to treasure, both now and in the future. You could make one for a birthday, as a way of celebrating a certain number of years of your friendship, as a leaving gift or simply to show someone how much you value them.

IDEAS TO GET YOU STARTED

Choose your book

If you love stationery, you'll enjoy this part of the process: heading to a craft shop to buy a notebook. You may want to ensure that the inside pages are quite plain, so that the things you add can take centre stage. The cover is also something to consider – if you are planning to paste it with pictures, the design won't really matter (although you may want to double check that it has a smooth surface for easy sticking), otherwise look for a cover that depicts something relevant to your friendship.

Collect your mementos

Depending on how in-depth you want your friendship book to be, this may be a project that you plan for a long time in advance, so that you can really stockpile a number of keepsakes from your outings and occasions together. This could include things like cinema tickets, pressed flowers and leaves, even sweet wrappers and notes you've written each other in class. You could print off screenshots of SMS conversations you've had or cut out photos of actors from a TV series you've watched together. You absolutely can't go wrong with pictures of the two of you together over the years, either – you could ask adults for help with collecting these, especially if your friendship goes way back to when you were little.

Think about how you want to mount these in your book. They could be chronological, clearly mapping out the timeline of your friendship, or perhaps organised in sub-categories like 'school', 'holidays' and 'parties'. Or they could be completely random. It's entirely up to you.

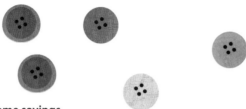

Gather some sayings

Is there a catchphrase the two of you always use? Or a favourite quote from a book or a film you both love? There are also many lovely and inspirational sayings about friendship. Pinterest is a good place to look online for one that has relevance to you and your BFF, or you could start with one of these:

* *Good friends are like stars: you don't always see them, but you know that they're always there.*
* *A good friend knows all your best stories; a best friend has lived them with you.*
* *Best friends are people you can do anything and nothing with, and still have the best time.*
* *A true friend knows your weaknesses, but shows you your strengths.*

Write some of these sayings in the pages of your book, whether on the same page as a memento or on a page of their own. There are tutorials online if you want to use a flowing, decorative look for your handwriting, but calligraphy pens are a fantastic 'cheat' and can give you a similar effect. If you struggle with your handwriting, though, don't worry – just print off the sayings you want to use and stick them in.

Add your own words and stories

Again, this can be anything you like. Perhaps you'll fill an entire page telling your friend why they are so special to you, or perhaps you'll jot down recollections alongside various things that you've stuck in. Next to a cinema ticket, for example, you might write: 'That person who was munching their popcorn really loudly!' Or next to a photo you could detail some of the things that you remember about the event that it has captured.

Decorate

Finish up by filling in the blank spaces with swirls, patterns, stickers, stamps, buttons and feathers – use anything that takes your fancy and makes your book as colourful and as fun as your friendship.

A good friend is like a four-leaf clover: hard to find and lucky to have.

ART FOR
THE HEART

Art can make you happy. So why not bring some of it into your own room?

It has been scientifically proven that looking at art can make you happy. Art will make you so happy, in fact, that the mere sight of a piece of artwork produces the same reaction in the brain as being in love. Perhaps that's why so many people have found themselves enamoured with the likes of Botticelli and Monet for centuries.

If visits to a gallery and looking at works of art can produce such a state of bliss in the brain, why not try to replicate those uplifting feelings in your own room? It's true you may not be hanging an original by Andy Warhol on your wall, but start in the right place and there are plenty of options to begin collecting and bringing that same sense of euphoria into your space.

It's worth noting that a love of art is not the same as a love of clothes or a pair of shoes – fashions come and go and tastes change. The connection is more emotional and lasts a lot longer than a liking for this season's latest trainers.

An artwork might remind you of a special time in your life, the way you felt at the time you bought it or a particular person. Robert Diament, director of online art shop countereditions.com, believes there's often a fine line between love and hate when you live with an artwork. 'Some works – in fact, I think the best ones – are ones that I constantly fall in and out of love with,' says Robert. 'I can switch from loving them to then feeling really irritated, almost as if they're challenging me. I never even knew this was possible before I lived with art, but the best art can really do that, it can provoke strong feelings just like an actual person can.'

The art world can be an intimidating one to enter, however. It has a reputation for big money and serious knowledge, but you don't have to be a professional – or a millionaire – to start your own collection. Most experts will tell you that you can start a collection by listening first and foremost to your heart, and there's something kind of beautiful in that.

HOW TO START A COLLECTION

Check Instagram to find up-and-coming artists

Instagram has opened up the art world to a brand-new audience. The visual online platform is a great place for artists to showcase their work and build a real connection with their followers and many buyers are now heading to the platform to find new pieces to purchase. Instagram also gives you a chance to see behind the scenes – whether it's the artist sharing what inspires them or the processes involved in creating pieces.

If you're stuck for where to start or feel overwhelmed by all the art-related content on the platform, try following contemporary galleries and art-fair accounts to find up-and-coming talent.

You can find editions that are more affordable than originals

Editions can be a great way to start collecting art. An edition is a copy of an original piece of artwork. Artists often create a small number of printed editions that they number and sign – they don't cost as much as an original, but they are still a valuable piece to own and are worth saving up for.

'SOME PEOPLE LOOK FOR A BEAUTIFUL PLACE.
OTHERS MAKE A PLACE BEAUTIFUL'

Hazrat Inayat Khan

Frame your travel mementos or pick up pieces on your travels

Collecting postcards from art galleries is a great way to start a personal collection. It might not be a ground-breaking collection of original artworks, but you will have a personal connection to them – they represent memories of exhibitions and galleries you've visited across the world. They're easy to frame, and you could alternate them in different areas of your room every few months, so you have your own rotating collection. Vintage maps, retro posters and old photographs are also often available at flea markets or antique fairs, all of which can help to add yet more personal flavour to your collection.

Take time to explore gallery and museum shops

Gallery shops are a great place to browse for prints and some even sell editions of pieces you may have seen on display. Try the Tate Modern in London, Hauser and Wirth in Somerset, Walker Art Gallery in Liverpool or the Scottish National Gallery in Edinburgh, to name a few.

Go to talks and listen to art-themed podcasts

Talks are a great way to learn and meet artists – go along and chat to as many as you can. If you can't make it to talks, try a podcast. Robert's Talk Art podcast with actor and art collector Russell Tovey includes interviews with artists and aims, in Robert's words, 'to get close to art'.

CLIMB THAT MOUNTAIN

Some tasks or goals can feel out of reach, as if you're standing at the bottom of a mountain and looking up at a faraway summit, but all you need to do is break the climb down rock-by-rock and soon you'll be on your way up

Set your sights on the summit

The first step is to be really clear about what it is you want to achieve. If you can see yourself at the summit then you're already getting closer. Find a quiet place where you can sit comfortably without being disturbed. Close your eyes and picture yourself achieving your goal or completing your task. Really visualise and feel it, imagine it's happening.

Give the image extra dimension. Imagine what people will say to you, how you will feel and what you will see around you once you reach the summit. Sit for a few moments and soak up the image. You can write down what you see, hear and feel afterwards as a reminder to keep you motivated.

Aim high but stay grounded

Now you can see your summit, it may still appear too much of a climb. If you break it down into much smaller steps, it becomes more achievable. You could even map out a series of milestones along the way so you can celebrate each time you pass one.

As strange as it might sound, planning in reverse can also provide a clearer view of how much time each phase of the project needs. Begin with the final step before you reach your summit. For example, if you have an essay to complete by a deadline, the last stage would be submitting the final draft, before that you'll need to refine a second draft, before that compose a first draft, then a skeletal structure and prior to that you'll need time for research.

Map the terrain ahead

Now you've outlined each step, take time to develop them one by one in more detail. Write an inventory of the resources and equipment you'll need, which could include anything from sports shoes to stationery, internet access or time to brainstorm ideas with friends.

The more prepared you are, the better equipped you'll be to navigate any obstacles that threaten to throw you off course. So grab something to write with and answer the following questions:

* How much time does each step need?
* What resources are required for the different stages?
* Do you know where to find all of these resources?
* Will you need support from anyone at any point?
* How could you team up with friends along the way?
* What obstacles might you face?
* How could you overcome these obstacles?

REACH YOUR GOALS

Brief your orienteering team

It's rare that a mountaineer completes a journey without assistance, so ask for any help you might need in advance. Let the people you spend the most time with know about your task before you begin so they're ready to support you.

What's more, a friend, parent, guardian or teacher can help you to develop new skills along the way. Say you're really good at maths and not so good at languages; if you just focused on numbers, your Spanish, Mandarin or French would never improve. This is an opportunity to explore new territory.

Don't forget your first-aid kit

Build room into your schedule to take time out if you feel tired. You could progress faster by pausing occasionally to recharge your energy reserves. The more exhausted you feel, the slower you'll advance and the more susceptible you'll become to feeling overwhelmed.

Be kind to yourself by resting to come back stronger, and checking in regularly at basecamp. Don't be afraid to go back to the drawing board at any point. This is your journey and it isn't a race. If you're feeling tired, take a moment to answer the following questions:

* How could I break my journey down into even smaller steps?
* Where do I need more time to complete a task?
* Are any extra resources required?
* Who could I ask for support to make this more manageable?
* What other activities could inspire or motivate me?

Celebrate reaching the summit

When you reach your summit, stop to celebrate your success and enjoy the view before rushing onto another task. Sometimes you have to get to the top before you can really see where you'd like to go next.

While you're up there, look back on how far you've come and acknowledge your achievement. Knowing what you're capable of will inspire you to pursue other goals in the future and to enjoy, understand and learn from any mini-successes and failures on the way. Share the good news with friends and family, thanking those who've helped you. Most of all, give yourself a big pat on the back to acknowledge all the effort you've put in.

TEEN Breathe

TEEN BREATHE is a trademark of Guild of Master Craftsman Publications Ltd

First published 2022 by Ammonite Press
an imprint of Guild of Master Craftsman Publications Ltd
Castle Place, 166 High Street, Lewes, East Sussex, BN7 1XU, United Kingdom

www.ammonitepress.com
www.teenbreathe.co.uk

Editorial: Susie Duff, Josie Fletcher, Catherine Kielthy, Jane Roe

Publisher: Jonathan Grogan
Designer: Jo Chapman

Words credits: Dawattie Basdeo, Claire Blackmore, Vicky H Bourne, Tracy Calder, Alice Carder,
Jenny Cockle, Charlie Cook, Claire Cook, Lorna Cowan, Kerry Dolan, Lorna Easterbrook, Laura
Gabrielle Feasey, Donna Finlay, Anne Guillot, Dr Sarah Maynard, Emma Newlyn, Jo Murphy, Jill Pelton,
Jo Porter, Sarah Rodrigues, Carol Anne Strange, Xenia Taliotis

Illustrations: Lou Baker Smith, Alessandra De Cristofaro, Nicola Ferrarese, Katerina Gorelik,
Beatrix Hatcher, Claire van Heukelom, Vanessa Lovegrove, Maria Mangiapane, Samantha Nickerson,
Sam Pernoski, Helma Speksnijder, Sara Thielker, Rachel Tunstall, Michelle Urra, Sarah Wilkins,
Shutterstock.com

Cover illustration: Charly Clements

ISBN 978 1 78145 470 1

A catalogue record for this book is available from the British Library

Colour reproduction by GMC Reprographics
Printed and bound in Turkey

AMMONITE
PRESS